EUROPE AND THE EVOLUTION OF THE INTERNATIONAL MONETARY SYSTEM

Institut Universitaire de Hautes Etudes Internationales
Collection d'Economie Internationale
1
International Economics Series

EUROPE AND THE EVOLUTION OF THE INTERNATIONAL MONETARY SYSTEM

Proceedings of the First Conference
of the

International Center for Monetary and Banking Studies

Edited by
Alexander K. Swoboda

1973
A. W. SIJTHOFF - LEIDEN
Institut Universitaire de Hautes Etudes Internationales
GENÈVE

ISBN 90 286 0173 2 (Sijthoff)

Foreword

Planned during the early part of the summer of 1971, the conference on Europe and the Evolution of the International Monetary System was held in Geneva on January 13-15, 1972. The conference was designed to meet two objectives. It aimed, first, at clarifying some of the fundamental choices open to an international monetary system that was increasingly showing signs of profound strain. In particular, the role of Europe in a system revolving around the dollar and the United States seemed to deserve careful attention. The conference attempted, in the second place, to enlist the collaboration of specialists from the academic, official, and private financial communities in the discussion of these issues and to explore the possibility of fostering permanent collaboration among these groups through the creation in Geneva of an International Center for Monetary and Banking Studies.

This volume gathers the papers presented at the conference. The United States measures announced on August 15, 1971 by President Nixon and the Smithsonian Agreement of December of that same year undoubtedly lent the choice of issues and the discussion a strong aura of topicality. Subsequent events and a re-reading of the papers suggest, however, that the issues that were debated at the conference are of far more than passing interest.

For more than ten years, the world has been on a dollar standard, to use an over-simplified but suggestive appellation. For a number of years, and on the whole, this system served its purpose well : in particular it facilitated the restructuring of the world economy and a rapid expansion of world trade. For a number of reasons, however, not least among them the re-emergence of stronger economic and political power outside the United States, the system has outlived its usefulness, and its general acceptability in its historical form. The logic of the dollar standard requires that the rest of the world accept and adjust itself to the rate of monetary expansion, and to a large extent, the rate of inflation chosen by the center country, the United States. The acceleration of monetary expansion and subsequently of inflation in the United States after 1966 thus became a first important factor undermining the stability of international monetary order. In addition, the consequent increase in the rate of dollar reserve accumulation by foreign monetary authorities gave rise to conflict as to asset choice and exacerbated the seigniorage problem, *i.e.* the tax that can be extracted by the United States by virtue of its position as the major issuer of international reserves. Finally, a fixed exchange-rate system such as the dollar standard can function properly only if confidence in the maintenance of the principal existing parities, especially that of the center currency in terms of an average of the rates of other major currencies, prevails. The system became particularly sensitive to a growing lack of confidence as capital could move more and more rapidly and massively from country to country.

The features, shortcomings, and probable future of the dollar standard and of some main alternatives are discussed by the contributors to Part II of this volume, "Europe and the System". The potential role of SDRs as an alternative to dollar reserves and as one of the means for funding the so-called dollar "overhang" are explored by Fritz Machlup. This overhang is also one of the issues discussed by Fred Bergsten who lists the features required of a reform plan that would in his view be acceptable to the United States, principally, adjustment through more frequent and more symmetric and automatic parity changes, elimination of the excess overhang and adequate liquidity growth. Richard Cooper strikes a cautionary note on the possibility of devising alternatives to the dollar standard that would restore symmetry in international monetary relations without instituting more profound changes in the system than those usually considered. In particular, he points to the problems created for consolidation of dollar balances by the deep asymmetries due to the sheer economic weight of the United States in the world economy and the role of the dollar in official and private transactions. Part II of this volume thus provides an analysis of some of the main shortcomings of the present system and of the contribution that increased symmetry in adjustment, consolidation of the overhang, greater reliance on an internationally created reserve asset and more exchange-rate flexibility could make to its reform. As Fritz Machlup notes, greater exchange-rate flexibility need not mean that the mode and rate of creation of international reserves becomes an irrelevant issue as long as the flexibility remains limited.

A pure dollar standard, a universal and symmetric system of fixed exchange rates based on SDRs, and freely floating rates of exchange among existing currencies are of course not the only possible alternative modes of international monetary organization. The formation of monetary blocs, in particular of a European currency area, has loomed large in discussions of the possible evolution of the international monetary system. Part III of this volume is devoted to the issues involved. These include the questions of whether European monetary union is feasible, whether it is desirable and what form it should take. Robert Triffin argues that European monetary integration is both feasible and desirable and that a European Fund, the functioning of which he spells out, and its gradual evolution into a European Reserve System could contribute much to its realization. Harry Johnson and Bela Balassa take a different stand. Johnson argues that the goal of economic integration may be better served by greater exchange-rate flexibility than by greater rigidity and that the likelihood of European monetary union is inversely related to the satisfactory performance of the dollar standard, itself a function of monetary stability in the United States. Balassa's survey of the actual history of the EEC's efforts and of evidence concerning individual European countries' preferences and actual trade-off possibilities as between inflation and unemployment lead him to conclude that progress towards economic and monetary union is likely to be much slower thant its advocates predict. Balassa then argues that limited exchange-rate flexibility within the European economic bloc would represent the most efficient organizing principle for regional monetary relations. Herman Wortmann takes issue with both Balassa and Johnson and argues that economic and monetary union is both feasible and compatible with a substantial degree of national political autonomy.

The last section of this volume contains two papers that deal with capital movements and the problems they pose for the future of the international monetary system. Marcus Fleming, after noting the recent increase in the volume and variability of capital movements, reviews the possibilities open for moderating their impact and indicates a preference for greater exchange-rate flexibility. Alexander Swoboda focusses on the relationship between capital movements and national and world money supplies with special reference to the role of the Eurodollar market and of alternative forms of international monetary organization. He argues that disruptive capital movements are mainly a symptom and not a cause of crises and offers some suggestions as to methods of increasing the stability of the system.

It will be obvious to the reader that the essays collected here do not aim at providing definite solutions to the many problems considered at the conference. They do, however, contribute to clarify a number of issues that tend to be systematically dodged in official discussion of international monetary reform. Less obviously, this volume does not entirely reflect the contribution the conference made to a better understanding of these issues and of the positions of various participants in the international money game. It is perhaps not unfair to say that the participants also learned much from the lively and constructive discussion among members of the three main groups represented at the conference, academics, officials, and specialists from the private sector.

In organizing the conference as well as in preparing this volume, we have incurred many debts of gratitude. The idea of combining the launching of an International Center for Monetary and Banking Studies with the organization of the conference originated in a conversation between Robert Mundell and the members of the organization committee of the Center (which also became the organization committee of the conference), namely, Pierre Keller, Nicolas Krul, and Alexander Swoboda. From an early stage, the organization committee had the great fortune of receiving the active support and kind encouragement of Federal Councillor Nello Celio, Head of the Department of Finance and Customs. Mr. Celio was kind enough to accept to deliver the opening address at the conference, the text of which constitutes Part I of this volume. The conference was organized in association with the Graduate Institute of International Studies whose director, Professor Jacques Freymond, supported and encouraged us from the very beginning. Materially, the conference was made possible by the financial support of a number of Swiss banks, notably Julius Bär & Co., Crédit Suisse, Ferrier, Lullin & Cie, Hentsch & Cie, Lombard, Odier & Cie, Pictet & Cie, Société de Banque Suisse and Union de Banques Suisses.

Whatever success the conference itself had was due mainly to the participants, authors of papers, discussants and session chairmen. As discussants, Baron Ansiaux, Leslie Dicks-Mireaux, Herbert Giersch, Milton Gilbert, Max Iklé, J. Kymmel, Alexandre Lamfalussy, and Kurt Richebächer helped create a useful and lively debate. The discussion was guided gently but firmly by three outstanding session chairmen, Alexandre Hay, Marius Holtrop, and Jacques Rueff.

In his opening address, Mr. Nello Celio fittingly reminds us that the problems discussed in this volume are not only technical economic ones but are also closely shaped by political events. The usefulness of this volume must ultimately lie in its contribution, however modest, to a better understanding of both the political and the economic issues involved in reform of the international monetary system. Only with such understanding can policy measures be the result of conscious choice rather than of the pressure of events, however much measures taken under pressure may later be rationalized as acts of enlightened statesmanship.

Geneva, April 1973 A. K. S.

Contents

Participants

Nello CELIO	Président de la Confédération ; Chef du Département des finances et des douanes
Baron ANSIAUX	Banque Nationale de Belgique
Franz E. ASCHINGER	Société de Banque Suisse
Roger AUBOIN	Genève
Nicolas BAER	MM. Julius Bär & Cie
Bela BELASSA	The Johns Hopkins University and IBRD
Pierre BARRE	Banque de France
Giorgio BASEVI	Università di Bologna
A. BATENBURG	Algemene Bank Nederland NV
C. Frcd BERGSTEN	The Brookings Institution
F. BOYER DE LA GIRODAY	Commission des Communautés européennes
René BUJARD	MM. Hentsch & Cie
Emil CLAASSEN	Université de Paris
Richard N. COOPER	Yale University
Gérard CURZON	Institut universitaire de hautes études internationales
Jean-Pierre DEMOLE	MM. Pictet & Cie
Leslie A. DICKS-MIREAUX	Bank of England
Kurt EKLOEF	Sveriges Riksbank

Paul FABRA	Le Monde
Raymond FERRIER	MM. Ferrier, Lullin & Cie
J. Marcus FLEMING	International Monetary Fund
Jacques FREYMOND	Institut universitaire de hautes études internationales
Herbert GIERSCH	Universität Kiel
Milton GILBERT	Bank for International Settlements
Alexandre HAY	Banque Nationale Suisse
Jean-Claude HENTSCH	MM. Hentsch & Cie
Marius W. HOLTROP	Former Governor of The Netherlands Bank
Max IKLE	Eidgenössische Bank
Harald JOERGES	Deutsche Bundesbank
Harry G. JOHNSON	The London School of Economics and Political Science and the University of Chicago
Sven JUNGHOLM	Svenska Arbetsgivare Föreningen
Pierre KELLER	MM. Lombard, Odier & Cie
E. S. KIRSCHEN	Université libre de Bruxelles
Nicolas KRUL	MM. Lombard, Odier & Cie
J. KYMMELL	Pierson, Heldring & Pierson
Alexandre LAMFALUSSY	Banque de Bruxelles
Jacques L'HUILLIER	Institut universitaire de hautes études internationales
Assar LINDBECK	University of Stockholm
Olivier LONG	GATT
Fritz MACHLUP	Princeton University and New York University
Hans MOESCHINGER	Banque Leu AG
Robert A. MUNDELL	University of Waterloo

Peter M. OPPENHEIMER	University of Oxford
Heinz PORTMANN	Neue Zürcher Zeitung
Kurt RICHEBACHER	Dresdner Bank
Jacques RUEFF	Paris
Pascal SALIN	Université de Paris
M. SANCHEZ-PEDRENO	Banque d'Espagne
Claude DE SAUSSURE	MM. Pictet & Cie
Samuel SCHWEIZER	Société de Banque Suisse
Claudio SEGRE	MM. Lazard Frères & Cie
Sergio SIGLIENTI	Banca Commerciale Italiana S.p.A.
Joao A. SIMOES DE ALMEIDA	Banco Totta y Açores
Alexander K. SWOBODA	Institut universitaire de hautes études internationales
Robert TRIFFIN	Yale University
John WATTS	Brown Brothers Harrimann & Co.
Philippe DE WECK	Union de Banques Suisses
Herman R. WORTMANN	Commission des Communautés européennes

PART I

INTRODUCTION

Opening Address

1

M. Nello CELIO
President of the Swiss Confederation

I

My colleagues of the Federal Council have asked me to convey their heartfelt wishes for the success of this meeting. The Swiss Government appreciate your tenacious attempts at clarifying, understanding and solving one of the most delicate problems of our times. They have asked me to convey their particular gratitude to those who have come from abroad to attend this conference on monetary problems, a conference that is to escape the pressure of political influence and private interests. Switzerland is committed to world cooperation, and Geneva is the symbol of this commitment. We are always happy to welcome and to be host to all those whose aim it is to serve mankind in a spirit of loyal dialogue and who meet on Swiss soil to try and work out constructive solutions to the problems of our times. Your presence here today undoubtedly reflects your shared belief in an international solidarity of minds and ideas. I am sure that it is this same belief that brought here numerous leaders and experts of the Swiss economy, and I am happy to welcome them too. I would like them to know that they enjoy our high esteem and I wish to thank them for the support they have given the Federal Council during the trying weeks we have just been through. Their support has been unreserved at times, and at other times critical. We welcome their criticism when it comes, for criticism often serves a Government better than disillusioned acceptance.

The Federal Council's deepest thanks go to the Graduate Institute of International Studies which is run by Professor Freymond with proverbial skill and distinction, to Professor Swoboda who has been the heart and soul of this meeting, and to the group of Swiss banks and, in particular, Geneva private banks without whose help it could not have taken place. It would be hard to think of a symposium theme of more burning concern both to Governments and the governed, a matter of more crucial interest to each of us, whatever his place in society, than current monetary issues.

II

I would like to begin by expressing a wish—and in this happy country of ours wishes are only hopes, not orders. Events, both recent and less recent, have shown that monetary issues are not only highly complex but also endemic. It would be mere daydream to hope for a final solution, one which would forever remain the right solution. Since changing external factors, both economic and political, constantly come into play, the best one can do is to keep aiming at greater stability and to readjust one's sights as events command. This is why I feel that it is very important that this conference's discussions, however useful in themselves, not remain without sequel. I hope that the views expressed at your meeting will fall on fertile soil and will bear fruit. Why not create, here in Switzerland, a Center for monetary studies ? It could be started on a modest scale, as would become a small country like ours. We might, in view of our neutrality, be less inclined than the larger nations to give a political bias to the study of a problem that requires first and foremost an objective approach, free of passion and of the need to assert or defend one's prestige.

The Federal Council would have good cause to rejoice if, besides the National Bank whose distinguished members act as our advisers and negotiators, an independent research Center were to be set up. This Center would enjoy the support of academic and business circles throughout the world ; it could be both an element and a symbol of Switzerland's share in the reconstruction of the world monetary system.

In making this suggestion, I believe I voice the unanimous view of the Federal Government. It always has been and will ever remain grateful to officials and especially to private groups and individuals for their efforts not only to make Switzerland's presence felt in international affairs but also to bear witness to our disinterested determination to help solve the difficult problems confronting the contemporary world. As you know, I have never attempted to conceal my own views and have always made it clear that I felt Switzerland should play an active role in international monetary organizations.

III

You will, Ladies and Gentlemen, have a lot to attend to during the next two days. You will be talking about the evolution of the world monetary system, about flexible exchange rates, European monetary union and the Eurodollar market, among many more topics. It would be impertinent of me to try and anticipate your discussions. I accepted the privilege of being with you tonight in order to learn, not to expose my limited knowledge to the fire of your able and critical minds.

Nevertheless, allow me to put forward a few thoughts concerning the symposium which is to begin tomorrow. For economic problems to be dealt with in depth, discussion must, of course, be carefully circumscribed. But, as one goes beyond purely technical matters, it becomes obvious that monetary problems are closely linked with a whole set of other issues and that certain conditions must be fulfilled if monetary mechanisms are to work properly. As a consequence, the elaboration of realistic and effective policies requires a comprehensive view of all relevant, political and economic factors. A policy, even though technically perfect, will remain worthless, if it is not sustained by political will. Any system can function effectively only if it fits properly into a political and economic framework. Take a problem which happens to be in all our minds, that of the future of currencies. That future is intimately bound with the ebb and flow of war and peace, whether present conflicts are soon to end or on the contrary are to be extended, whether the major powers spend huge sums on war abroad or whether they pull out their troops and put an end to their fighting, if only because all these main alternatives of foreign policy have a direct impact on the budgets and foreign commitments of the countries concerned.

That the whole world is going through a crisis and that contemporary societies are undergoing transformations which explain the instability of international equilibrium is, I think, obvious. It is, however, harder to realize how widespread, serious and dangerous this crisis is. Again, the world's economies and public spending cannot but be significantly affected not only by the major powers' political commitments and their psychological side-effects but also by these same powers' disengagements. Of course, all major events—the main developments of world politics, employment policies, inflation trends, capital flows, to cite but a few—have considerable bearing on monetary phenomena. However, the considerable role of international security and the crucial problem of armament and of the major powers' defence responsibilities deserve to be singled out in this context. Efforts to promote world security, to limit the arms race, to reduce nuclear expenditure, aside from their bearing on the balance of fear, are bound to have favourable effects on money and trade.

IV

All the above factors obviously have direct effects upon the structure of balances of payments. Because of the huge sums involved the choice between war and peace has more considerable monetary implications than ever before in history. This is all the more important since the arguments of power politics typically take precedence over the technical arguments of those who must eventually find ways to settle the economic and monetary bill. This should not make us forget a second and economic factor. In the conclusion to his book "Magie des Geldes", Schacht wrote : "The magic of money is a constant source of problems. These keep changing and experience has taught us that a given system only works in a given set of circumstances. New circumstances call for new thinking and policies. These new ideas can have but one aim : to keep money sound and healthy".

The market economy too is showing symptoms of crisis. I need not remind a gathering of eminent experts that one can no longer rely on the play of automatic stabilizing or countervailing forces. The spectacular growth we have witnessed since the war has brought in its wake problems we cannot solve and with which the private sector can no longer cope on its own. I shall not dwell tonight on environmental issues nor on the gradual shifting of attention from the myth of profit towards pursuit of the quality of life. There is no doubt that our society is going through an inner transformation whose consequences we cannot foresee. I do not claim that the world we live in shall be better in years to come but I am sure that it shall be different. Suffice it to say, here, that the free world's economy has been following some dangerous paths of late, shaking men's minds and hence society as a whole in the process. In spite of the endeavours of international meetings, of the creation of broader markets, in spite of energetic action by governments, we have failed to achieve a fair sharing of burdens, and to insure reasonable behaviour on the part of the public. We have thus been unable to stop the inflation which has caused and still is causing so much harm both political and economic. Inflation is increasingly tending to become the chief enemy of democracy, of freedom and order. Most industrial countries have, it is true, achieved growth and full employment, but they have had to pay a heavy price for it, inflation. They have suffered domestic inflation first, as a result of the urge to meet all claims and expectations at once and fully ; and then imported inflation due to the interpenetration of our economies. Neither the larger economic powers, such as the United States, nor the socialist countries have been able to control this plague. The myth of growth together with the wish to secure the best possible conditions for development, on one hand, popular demands and demagogy, on the other hand, have made us lose all sense of discipline. And without discipline even the best monetary systems will fail to function properly.

Governments, in spite of all the measures they have taken, have been unable to defeat speculation. That is one of the causes of monetary crises. Recent symptoms indicate that the December 1971 crisis will not be the last.

The myth of growth, so dear to public authorities, to employers and to unions, has raised expectations well above what our economies can bear. These demands have, it is true, been met so far thanks to the great flexibility of credit and money, but at the price of economic imbalance and an overdose of inflation. Unless we put bounds to our greed, unless we stop overstraining the machine, it will be hard to defeat inflation, short of a general recession due to a collective abdication of the will to work and to take risks. And that would be a case of circumstances bringing about a bitter victory without any share of merit on our part. I have often been told it was wrong to use monetary measures in order to regulate business cycles ; I endeavour to heed this advice, even though I am not wholly convinced of its soundness. There are certain ills you must try to cure by unfamiliar means when normal remedies fail.

Be that as it may, economic stability is an essential component of monetary policy— and the reverse is true. It is also an indispensable condition of the survival of our market economy. There is no doubt that inflation signals the beginning of the disintegration of a free economy. We saw this clearly when certain countries instituted price and wage controls, together with an incomes policy. Such measures eliminate the natural price mechanism which is the essential component of a market economy. It is, therefore, necessary that all those who wish to safeguard the free market system understand the need to take corrective measures against inflation including, if required, restrictive measures, if we are not to find ourselves forced some day by the twin pressures of opinion and of circumstances to set up a state-controlled economy which would hardly be compatible with the structures and the spirit of western society.

Should monetary policy be used in the battle against inflation ? Whenever inflation is a case of too much money chasing too few goods, I believe the answer is yes. However, it must be stressed that international cooperation is indispensable in this context ; for no country is able to control international capital movements on its own, especially when states insist on sending unwanted hot money back to each other.

A small country such as ours, with its extremely well-developed banking system, has every reason to fear the huge accumulation of liquid capital which might at any moment disturb its internal monetary, political and economic order. Contemporary society cannot tolerate the constant threat of uncontrolled forces. In this context, international monetary discipline suffers today from the lack of sanctions against countries in payments deficit, a deficit that is itself a source of inflation especially when currencies are not convertible. The situation is particularly complex for Switzerland even in the context of a European solution to the international monetary problem as we have an asymmetrical balance of trade with a considerable deficit vis-à-vis our Common Market trade partners and a surplus with the dollar and other currency areas.

The depreciation of money has in the long run been lethal to all political systems. Balance and economic order (as evidenced by a reasonable growth rate and claims proportionate to the growth of productivity) are essential to a country's development. It is on such foundations, together with the liberalization of trade in industrial products, that the world economy, which so nearly collapsed, should be reconstructed. The public as well as the private sector must seek to eliminate all sources of inflation, in particular through relentless screening of all public expenditure. Inflation leads to a geometrical progression of public spending whenever one attends to its effects and fails to attack its causes.

Placing a ceiling on public spending, without, of course, neglecting the social obligations of a community committed to progress, means that wealth is allocated to production, in other words to the technical and economic development of the country. Wealth should be used to improve standards of living, not to pamper pernickety bureaucrats. Controlling credit and public spending will not suffice in itself both to stimulate the economy and to control inflation. Our chief aim should be to balance production, economic resources and social demands. I speak, alas, from personal experience. I have always felt, without being able to prove it, that our society is no longer producing enough wealth to undertake the huge investments required today, especially in the fields of health and technology. The same imbalance will appear some day—there are, indeed, signs of it already—in the monetary and economic fields. The enormous expansion of technology unmatched by a simultaneous development of real values has brought in its wake the monetary disequilibrium that is at the root of many of our present troubles. Our dilemma is this : if men want to consume more and yet to work and to produce less, if what they consume, being ever more perfected must cost ever more, we shall have willy-nilly to accept restrictions, a result that is the precise opposite of that originally sought.

V

Forgive me these few digressions. I had no new wisdom to impart but merely wished to remind you that all problems are linked. Only a comprehensive view, however difficult to achieve, can lead to constructive solutions to general economic problems. In addition to this global view of problems, constructive solutions require adequate behaviour on the part of economic man who will be the master of his fate only if he lets himself be guided by his mind more than by his appetites.

I once again bid you welcome in the name of the Federal Council. I thank you all for coming, and wish you a most successful meeting.

PART II

EUROPE AND THE SYSTEM

The Expanded Role of SDRs and the Possibilities of an SDR Standard

2

Fritz MACHLUP
Princeton University and New York University

The SDR—Special Drawing Rights, issued by the International Monetary Fund to participating member countries—has really come up in the financial world. It has been nominated for functions which a couple of years ago no one had thought it could or should be capable of performing. The SDR has been proposed as a successor to the present reserve currencies, particularly to all the dollars now held by national monetary authorities ; as a successor to gold as the ultimate official reserve asset into which currencies should be convertible ; and as the common denominator by which all currencies should be defined or in which their official par values should be stated. This ambitious career was not foreseen by even the most friendly of the good fairies that came to present their gifts and wishes when the SDR was born, let alone by the unfriendly fairies who predicted a rather dim future for the bastard child. All these fairy wishes can be found recorded in the minutes of the Annual Meeting of the International Monetary Fund held in Rio de Janeiro in September 1967, and similarly in those of the Meeting held in Washington in September 1969.

My task today is to examine the qualifications of the SDR for the jobs for which it has been recommended. My own qualifications as an examiner of the qualifications of SDR are perhaps attested to by my monographic study published in 1968 under the title *Remaking the International Monetary System.*[1] I neither expect nor assume that every one has read my booklet and, hence, I shall have to repeat a few things—a very few only—which I wrote there.

THE CHARACTERISTICS OF SDRs

The original intention was that SDRs would be a supplementary reserve asset, replacing, not existing currency reserves or existing gold

[1] Fritz Machlup, *Remaking the International Monetary System,* Baltimore, The Johns Hopkins Press, with the Committee for Economic Development, 1968.

reserves, but increases of currency or gold reserves. It was expected that there would be no further net increases in monetary gold and that the net additions of dollars in monetary reserves would decline and soon come to an end. With these assumptions, only two types of reserves would be subject to augmentation : one, the countries' reserve positions with the Fund through increased drawings made on the basis of quinquennial increases of quotas and, two, the annual allocations of SDRs.

The essential characteristics of the allocation of SDRs are the following :

— they are gratis reserves in the sense that the countries to which they are allocated have neither to earn them through surpluses in their balance of payments nor surrender any assets in exchange for them nor consider them as debts to be repaid (except in the case of liquidation) ;
— they are not debts, either of the IMF or of anybody else : they are, therefore, assets of the holder without being liabilities of anybody (thus resembling in this respect the stocks of monetary gold) ;
— they are, although defined as equivalents of a certain weight of gold, not convertible into gold or any other assets ;
— they are not "backed" or "covered" by any other asset ;
— they are simply drafts that can be exchanged for convertible currencies held by countries designated by the Fund, because of their generally strong reserve position, as possible drawees (recipients of the drafts).

SIGNIFICANCE OF THE PRINCIPLES OF SDR CREATION

My list of particulars or characteristics was offered here not as an enumeration of defects, though some old-fashioned monetary experts may think so. To be sure, the non-debt character of the SDR, its non-convertibility, and the lack of cover have all been cited as serious shortcomings, fatal weaknesses, or mortal sins. In contradistinction, I praised these characteristics as perfectly sensible and most desirable, and I commended the innovating officials for accepting the long overdue breakthrough in monetary institutional practice. Let me quote three sentences from my book : "Money needs takers, not backers ; the takers accept it, not because of any backing, but only because they count on others accepting it from them. The myth of backing is dead. It was buried in Rio de Janeiro on 29 September 1967." I must now add some apprehension that the ghost of the dead myth is still making its midnight rounds and frightens some of the grown-up children. (It seems especially terrifying to gnomes.)

Most academic economists are amused, not frightened, by the antics of the ghost. But a good many political economists still dislike the first of the characteristics on my list : the gratis allocation of the SDRs. There are some who regard free gifts to wealthy nations as immoral (even if they impose no costs on anybody) and would favor such gifts only to poor countries ; there are others who would prefer the issuance of official reserves as loans rather than as gifts. I cannot here take the time to repeat my defense of the principle of gratis allocation to all participating countries ; but I should not fail to point to the most important advantage of gifts over loans. If money, international or national, is created by granting loans, it can also be destroyed by repayments of loans ; when repayments exceed new borrowings, the stock of money is reduced. (Irving Fisher saw in such periodic "debt deflations" the main cause of the "credit cycle" with its crises and depressions.) If destruction of monetary reserves is to be avoided, reserves should not be created by extensions of repayable loans but, instead, by free allocations.

The reasons for providing for annual increases in total monetary reserves are as strong as ever. To be sure, countries want reserves in order to be able to finance deficits in their balance of payments ; but the creation of new reserves prevents some deficits from occurring and reduces those that it cannot prevent. Most countries—except those that have experienced excessive increases in reserves in preceding months and years—do not want their reserves to decline and they prefer to see them grow year after year. If total reserves are not growing, the surpluses of some countries impose deficits on other countries ; attempts to avoid these deficits take the form of credit restraints, trade restrictions, capital embargos, and exchange controls. The total of surpluses (calculated on the basis of official reserve transactions) can exceed the total of deficits to the extent that new reserves are created. Reserve creation, by keeping deficits smaller than they would be without it, serves to reduce the countries' propensity to restrict international flows of goods, services, and capital. And this is of eminent importance.

The arguments for annual creation and free allocation of monetary reserves remain valid even after the dollar flood of 1971 ; and SDRs are a most suitable instrument for this purpose.

SDRs AS MAJOR RESERVE ASSET

From the acceptance of the Rio Agreement in September 1967, to the activation of the SDR facility in January 1970, and indeed even later, not a few commentators expressed serious doubts that SDRs would ever become a reserve asset acceptable to national monetary authorities. It would be tempting to compile a list of the doubting Thomases and the reasons for their skepticism.

In contrast with these pessimistic views, I foresaw the possibility of a bright future for SDRs. Although I expected that SDRs in 1970 would be no more than 3 per cent of total reserves, I held that ten years later SDRs would have attained first place among the official monetary reserve assets of the world. This now appears to be even more likely, especially if a large part of existing reserve currencies is to be exchanged into SDRs, newly issued for this purpose, as proposed by several governors of the Fund. I am in favor of funding proposals but would prefer to have existing currency reserves exchanged into IMF deposits. I would, accordingly, anticipate first place among monetary reserves to be attained by the whole group of IMF issues, including deposits, but not by SDRs alone.

My present view is that SDRs will (or should) share top ranking with IMF deposits, that reserve currencies will not completely disappear from official holdings, and that gold will have come from first place to last place among the reserve assets in a not too distant future. I must now explain why I want Fund deposits rather than SDRs to be the asset for which currency reserves should be exchanged.

EXCHANGING EXCESS DOLLAR RESERVES INTO SDRs OR IMF DEPOSITS

For a good many years proposals have been made to remove currencies from official monetary reserves. We may recall the plans of Keynes, Triffin, Maudling, Bernstein and many others, all proposing an exchange of currencies into other assets, preferably deposit claims against the Fund. At the annual meeting of the IMF in 1971 several governors proposed the exchange of official holdings of dollars and sterlings into SDRs.

I fully share the conviction of these proponents that the excess holding of dollars and pounds in official reserves should be mopped up through a large funding operation. We may conceive of several workable techniques by which such funding may be achieved. We might, if time permitted, compare a few of these techniques in greater detail. At this moment I shall concentrate on arguing against an exchange of excess currency reserves into SDRs, and in favor of their exchange into deposit claims against the Fund.

My reasons for this preference are as follows :

- the essential characteristics of SDRs as non-debt assets not covered by anything should be preserved ;
- the creation of SDRs against surrender of dollars or sterling would create a claim of the depositor and a debt of the depository ;
- the currencies received by the latter, or the assets into which the currencies were to be funded, would constitute backing or cover for the SDRs issued ;

— thus the principle of SDR creation would be adulterated and we would have two kinds of SDRs, some uncovered non-debts, others covered liabilities of the Fund.

Such an adulteration of the principle of SDRs may put in jeopardy the important function of the SDR facility as the source of annual increases of reserves through free allocations to monetary authorities.

The alternative proposal of exchanging dollars into IMF deposits would have none of these disadvantages. IMF deposits would be a new type of reserve asset in addition to those now in existence. We need not fear the operation of Gresham's Law with respect to the three different assets issued by the IMF. Still less need we fear that Gresham's Law would operate with respect to the increasingly insignificant stocks of monetary gold. As a matter of fact, it may be desirable to assure the usefulness of monetary gold by providing for its (voluntary) exchange into IMF deposits. (If the price of gold in the free market should appreciably increase, it might be decided that the Fund eventually begin selling its gold—in small instalments—at a profit, which can be used for additional financing of development aid.)

MAKING SDRs THE COMMON DENOMINATOR FOR PAR VALUES OF CURRENCIES

Several governors of the Fund have discussed the possibility of using the unit of SDR as a common denominator for stating the par values of currencies. In view of the fact that SDRs are now defined in weights of gold, the proposal seems to make little practical difference. None the less, monetary authorities may wish to continue the "phasing out" of gold by replacing it also in the function of common denominator in fixing par values of their currencies.

Difficulties of definition may tax the imagination of lawyers. For the economist no such difficulty exists : in the mode of Gertrude Stein, "a unit is a unit is a unit"—and the unit may be a pure abstraction. Thus there would be no problem in expressing all par values in terms of a Fund unit. It would be awkward to call it SDR, since also the general account of the IMF and the deposit claims against the IMF should all be denominated in the same units. "Fondor" strikes me as a good name for the unit.

The hope has been expressed that the replacement of gold by SDRs as common denominator for par values would provide more symmetry in the positions of different currencies and do away with the special position of the dollar. The dollar could then be devalued or upvalued in terms of SDR or Fund units like any other currency. Alas, this is a fallacy. The lack of symmetry is not a question of the choice of denominator but is due to several facts of our financial life. The most pertinent of these are, one, that the dollar is the most convenient international transactions currency and, two, that the dollar is generally used as official intervention currency. As long as monetary authorities intervene in the foreign-exchange markets by selling and buying dollars, the dollar remains in an asymmetrical position.

This position is essentially the logical corollary of the fact that there can be only n-1 exchange rates for n currencies. If n-1 countries intervene in dollars at rates which they themselves determine, the United States can neither raise nor lower the external exchange value of the dollar. The United States can devalue or revalue the dollar only with the cooperation of the other countries. A set of rules with sanctions will have to be developed to enforce the necessary cooperation.

One may argue that all other countries would respect any change in par value (in terms of SDR, gold, or anything else) announced for the dollar by the United States, and would always adjust their intervention rates to conform with that announcement. If they did, they would be obeying a "rule" in a system of perfect cooperation. But would they? Would Japan or France have accepted a devaluation of the dollar if the United States had "announced" it on 15 August 1971? Surely not.

Alternatively, one may reject the view that the United States must passively accept the pattern of exchange rates which other countries determine by their interventions in the foreign-exchange markets. If the United States finds any of these rates seriously undervalued in relation to the dollar, it could start intervening, buying the currency in question at a higher price. Since such an exchange-rate war would lead to unlimited profits for arbitrageurs and perpetual inflationary money creation in the warring countries, an economically weaker country would have to capitulate sooner or later and accept the devaluation of the dollar. Thus, the denial of the need for international cooperation turns out to be in fact a confirmation of the thesis that cooperation may have to be imposed on those who want to go on imposing an overvaluation of the dollar on a "benign" United States.

An interesting suggestion in this connection has recently been made by Professor John Williamson.[2] If the United States wanted to reduce or remove an enduring payments deficit by devaluing its overvalued dollar, but other countries insisted on perpetuating the overvaluation of the dollar by declaring parallel devaluations of their currencies (in terms of gold or SDRs) and thus continued to purchase dollars at unchanged exchange

[2] John Williamson, *The Choice of a Pivot for Parities,* Essays in International Finance, No. 90, Princeton, International Finance Section, November 1971.

rates—too high for restoring balance—the Fund should issue sufficient amounts of SDRs to enable the United States to buy back the dollars being accumulated by surplus countries. These issues of SDRs would make it possible for other countries to go on having their surpluses and for the United States to remove its deficit. (The deficit would be "removed" if the allocation of SDRs is entered above the line in the balance of payments ; it would be "financed" if the receipt of the SDRs is entered below the line.) When other countries eventually get tired of exchanging their goods, services, and securities for ever increasing piles of SDRs, they may decide to accept a devaluation of the dollar.

An interesting aspect of Williamson's suggestion is that *more* SDRs are to be issued when more dollars flow into foreign reserves. This is in sharp contrast to the recommendations of other experts, who would issue *less* SDRs when more dollars swell the reserves of other countries.

MAKING SDRs THE OBJECT OF CONVERTIBILITY OF OTHER RESERVE ASSETS

At present the dollar is inconvertible. No matter how much some of the monetary authorities press for resumption of convertibility, the dollar must remain inconvertible as long as the vast mass of dollars is held by other monetary authorities. There cannot even be an approach to convertibility until the existing dollar holdings have been funded, mopped up or locked in ; perhaps provisional arrangements can be made for conditional convertibility or exchange-value guarantees limited to dollars acquired after 18 December 1971 (or an even later date). The only reason for such interim arrangements would be to encourage the monetary authorities of the financially most important countries to declare that they would defend the new floor price of the dollar no matter how many dollars were offered to them. Such a declaration would inspire private holders of dollars with sufficient confidence to hold on to their dollar balances and not to be panicked into a renewed flight from the dollar. (Incidentally, if the countries had agreed to a system of limited adjustments of central rates or par values—"crawling pegs"—the new pattern would have been more credible than the presumably fixed parities with a fixed floor only 2 1/4 per cent below these parities.)

Long-term arrangements for convertibility can become effective only after the great mopping-up and locking-in of the excess holdings of dollars (acquired before 15 August or 18 December 1971) have been completed. Mopping-up would be preferable to locking-in, at least from the point of view of the dollar-holding national authorities. Blocked or locked-in currency reserves can hardly be considered liquid monetary assets, unless special arrangements secure their transferability to other countries when their present holders are in deficit positions. In any case, the exchange of official excess holdings of dollars into Fund deposits denominated in Fund units would be more appropriate from the point of view of international liquidity.

When the official excess holdings of dollars are out of the way, dollars newly acquired by national monetary authorities can be made convertible into SDRs (or also into reserve positions with the Fund and deposits with the Fund). The new convertibility may still raise problems with regard to the large dollar balances held by private foreigners. These are now estimated to run to about $18 billion, with their "normal" size estimated to be about $25 billion at the present volume of international transactions. Can the United States reasonably undertake an obligation to convert official holdings of dollars into SDRs (or into claims against the Fund), if large amounts of privately held dollars may come onto the market at the slightest provocation—crises of confidence—and may have to be absorbed by monetary authorities, which in turn will present them for conversion? I would answer this question affirmatively only if the new international monetary system provides for greater flexibility of both interest rates and exchange rates.

A large speculative outflow of funds from the United States and excess supply of dollars in the foreign-exchange markets can be stemmed if interest rates for dollars rise sufficiently above those for other currencies and if the exchange rate for the dollar can fall sufficiently to make people anticipate a strong recovery of the dollar in subsequent months. A band of only 4 1/2 per cent, that is, 2 1/4 per cent up or down from the center, is probably not enough for this purpose. I stick to my recommendation of a band of 5 or 6 per cent, that is, 2 1/2 or 3 per cent around a center (parity) that can glide up or down with maximum changes of 1 per cent at a time and 2 or 3 per cent cumulatively over any twelve-month period. These speed limits for changes in parities and exchange rates can reduce the threat of speculative movements of liquid funds and can facilitate the adjustments to divergent trends in structural and monetary developments in different countries.

THE COEXISTENCE OF CONVERTIBILITY AND FLEXIBILITY

If limited flexibility of exchange rates is necessary for the promise of convertibility to be honest and credible, why, one may ask, is convertibility needed at all? If the exchange rate of the dollar is flexible, will monetary authorities be willing to acquire dollars in any large amounts? How can one expect a central bank to acquire large amounts of dollars at or near an agreed par of exchange if the rate at which the dollars can be converted into SDRs may be reduced before the dollars can be presented to the United States ?

The answers to these questions presuppose comprehension of the fact that "limited flexibility" may mean greater stability of exchange rates than that which exists under "fixed parities". Fixed parities are adjusted from one day to another by as much as 8, 12, or 16 per cent, and even more. In contrast to these jumping parities, gliding parities (or "crawling pegs") under a system of limited flexibility can be changed by only one per cent at a time, and by only 2 or 3 per cent over a year. Hence, if the rule is obeyed, the risk of acquiring and holding dollars is smaller under a system of greater flexibility than under one of rigidity of par values ; and convertibility is more easily maintained than with allegedly fixed parities.

I realize, of course, that convertibility (into SDRs or any other kind of reserve asset) would make no sense under a system of freely flexible exchange rates. Such a system would have no par values, no interventions in the foreign-exchange markets, no official acquisitions of dollars or any other foreign currencies and, hence, no conversions of currencies acquired. But we are not talking now about a system of freely flexible rates, because we all realize that such a system will not exist in the foreseeable future. We are talking about managed, limited flexibility. Such a system will include official interventions, official acquisitions of dollars, and hence, arrangements for converting dollars so acquired into other reserve assets (such as SDRs). The only alternatives to convertibility of this kind would be guarantees for the maintenance of the exchange value or purchasing power of the dollars acquired and held by the authorities of foreign countries.

THE "SDR STANDARD"

In the title of my paper appear the words "possibilities of an SDR standard". I have not used this expression up to now. I have avoided it because it has no clear meaning. I now want to expose the ambiguity of the phrase.

Adoption of the "SDR standard" may mean any of the following things :

(1) The SDR, or a unit of SDR, is the standard of value in which the people—businessmen, government officials, and perhaps also households—in the countries that have adopted that system calculate and compare the exchange values of goods and services.

(2) The SDR is the unit of account in which, in international transactions, prices, claims, debts, and payments are expressed.

(3) The SDR is the common denominator for stating, fixing, and refixing the par values of different currencies.

(4) SDRs are the most important asset held in the monetary reserves of the financially most important countries.

(5) SDRs are the reserve asset into which currencies are convertible under rules adopted by the major countries.

(6) The amounts of SDRs held as reserve by the monetary authority of a country determine the supply of its national money, or the increase in its SDR reserve determines the increase in its money supply.

Meaning (1) may be rejected out of hand (because it is inconceivable that the SDR will become the general standard of value). Meaning (6) may be excluded as too unlikely ever to become relevant. This leaves four possible meanings : the SDR may serve as the international unit of account, as the common denominator for setting par values, as the most important reserve asset, and as the asset into which currencies are made convertible. These four functions are independent of one another ; any one can possibly be performed without any of the others. Hence, the expression "SDR standard" would always require specification of the meaning in which it is used, and this would take more time than to state the function or functions which the SDR is really supposed to serve.

International Monetary Reform: A Viewpoint from the United States

3

C. Fred BERGSTEN
The Brookings Institution

The world stands today on a pure dollar standard. The dollar is the dominant currency in private financial transactions throughout the world. It is thus the currency in which national monetary authorities must carry out the bulk of their intervention in the exchange markets. Yet the United States will not convert dollars into U.S. reserve assets, does not intervene in the markets to maintain the new dollar parity, and will not offer exchange-rate guarantees through the swap network or Roosa bonds as in the past.

Thus other countries only have the choice between holding any dollars which may accrue to them and taking action themselves to eliminate such dollar holdings through appreciation of their own currencies or erection of controls against capital inflows. The elimination of the overvaluation of the dollar, brought about by the exchange rate realignment agreed to on 18 December 1971, eliminated one major threat to the economic viability of this pure dollar standard. Success of the current U.S. effort to bring its internal inflation under control, relative to inflation in the other major countries, would eliminate the other major threat. Indeed, the world role of the dollar had been continuing to expand rapidly anyway—despite the relative decline in U.S. world power, mismanagement of the U.S. domestic economy in the last half of the 1960s, the persistence of sizable deficits in the U.S. balance of payments and growing overvaluation of the dollar, the creation of an alternative reserve asset in Special Drawing Rights, and despite even the suspension of gold convertibility and devaluation. It is little wonder, then, that the dollar standard option should now look quite viable.

Superficially, this situation appears quite attractive from the standpoint of the United States. There is no external constraint on U.S. domestic economic policy. There is no pressure to tighten the present controls over capital outflows and government expenditures abroad in order to protect U.S. reserves ; they could even be lifted with impunity. Indeed, the United States can now avoid the political risks of taking *any* adjustment initiatives, acting only when—as on 15 August 1971—there is domestic political *gain* in doing so. It is quite likely that preservation of this new status quo will become increasingly appealing in the United States as its implications become more widely understood.

Nevertheless, it would be a disastrous error for the United States to seek to keep the world on a pure dollar standard. Such dollar hegemony is politically, and therefore economically, impossible for the longer run without over-all U.S. political and economic hegemony—which no longer exists, and will not be achieved again in the future. Other major countries would simply not accept U.S. financial domination in a world where they have already demonstrated both their ability and their desire to be full partners in endeavors ranging from negotiations with the Soviet Union through management of collective defense to determination of the amount of annual additions to world reserves. Europe, at least, would seek an alternative to the dollar and monetary duopoly could develop in the most destructive possible manner. Even if Europe *failed* to find a viable alternative for a while, the resulting acrimony would plague and indeed jeopardize economic, and eventually political, relations across the Atlantic.

But neither should the United States be willing to shoulder the responsibilities incumbent on a single key currency country, and to accept the resultant sacrifices of its own national sovereignty, without the requisite power and the "cooperation" of other countries which comes only with political domination. The great lesson for the United States and the dollar from the similar historical experience of the United Kingdom and sterling is to foresee in time the need to reduce gradually the world financial role of its key *currency* to maintain an equilibrium with its over-all world position as a key *country*. Such foresight is difficult, since tradition dies hardest in matters monetary and simple inertia prolongs the international status of a currency far beyond the dictates of the objective situation.

BETTER ADJUSTMENT

However, major changes will be needed in the monetary system to induce the United States to give up the benefits of the currently prevailing pure dollar standard and to resume dollar convertibility and its other international monetary obligations. Even greater changes will be needed if the United States is to agree to finance future deficits, in at least its basic balance of payments, with reserve assets as other countries are generally obliged to do. The most important change is the institution of an effective adjustment mechanism. Heretofore, from the standpoint of the United States, the adjustment system has been fatally marred by two paradoxes.

First, the United States has the least open economy to international transactions in the non-Communist world. It is thus the country in which exchange-rate changes have the greatest comparative advantage among alternative adjustment techniques. From the standpoint of maximum economic efficiency and political feasibility, the United States should perhaps even adjust its exchange rate *more* frequently than the other major countries. Yet, in large part because of the international roles of the dollar, the United States is the one country which has been unable to unilaterally change its own exchange rate at all.

Second, the United States has run persistent balance-of-payments deficits and has been continually exhorted "to put its house in order" ; yet, the exchange-rate changes initiated by other countries prior to 1971 produced a steady *upvaluation* of the dollar. This is because the monetary system generally has placed great pressure on deficit countries to adjust, but little pressure on surplus countries to do so, and because it has discouraged small parity changes in favor of large changes to occur only when "fundamental disequilibrium" has clearly developed. The result has been a quadruple bias against the dollar : currencies frequently succumb to the pressure to devalue, but infrequently to the pressure to revalue ; devaluations tend to be larger than necessary, to prevent speculation against further devaluations of the same currency ; any single devaluation tends to induce additional devaluations by other countries, because they both fear for their competitive positions and find it politically easier to devalue in company with others ; and revaluations tend to be smaller than necessary, since countries are even less fearful of pressures for additional revaluations than they are susceptible to pressures to move upward in the first place.[1]

Thus the United States has been unable to initiate effective adjustment itself, and its adjustment needs have often, and on balance, been affected perversely by the initiatives of other countries. The new adjustment mechanism will have to effectively resolve both problems to be acceptable to the United States.

It can hope to do so only by incorporating an internationally agreed set of criteria indicating when exchange rate changes are needed, which all countries—including the United States—will have both the right and responsibility to honor under penalty of sanctions applied by the international community as a whole against flagrant violations. The basic rule should be that exchange rates change to resolve "dilemma" cases : revaluation when a country runs a payments surplus with its domestic economy near full employment, devaluation when payments deficits coincide

[1] For a more complete analysis, see the author's "The United States and Greater Flexibility of Exchange Rates" in *Approaches to Greater Flexibility of Exchange Rates : The Burgenstock Papers,* arranged by C. Fred Bergsten, George N. Halm, Fritz Machlup, and Robert V. Roosa and edited by George N. Halm, Princeton, N.J., Princeton University Press, 1970 ; especially pp. 68-70.

with high unemployment. Domestic macroeconomic policy, of course, continues to be the proper remedy for "non-dilemma" cases : internal expansion in response to domestic unemployment coupled with payments surpluses, internal disinflation in response to excessive domestic inflation coupled with payments deficits.

In any given situation it may be difficult to distinguish between "dilemma" and "non-dilemma" cases. This is particularly true when domestic economies suffer from the purely internal dilemma of high unemployment and rapid inflation, as several now do. A schematic set of guidelines to deal with these more complex cases, which distinguishes between the proper responses of relatively open and relatively closed economies, can be found in Annex 1.

The difficulty of implementing such guidelines, even if they were agreed upon, should not be underestimated. Indeed, countries would be able to challenge the international assessment of their situation, or could try to convince others that actions already taken are adequate. Nevertheless, any meaningful guidelines would point clearly to the major problem cases which could disrupt the system (and the internal economy of the country in question) if left unattended, for instance the extreme undervaluation of the Japanese yen for an extended period prior to August 1971. Such guidelines, implemented through strong IMF leadership and backed by the threat of action by the entire international community, could have promoted adequate yen revaluations in plenty of time to help forestall the need for actions such as those taken by the United States on August 15.

Some will view this proposal as utopian, with its apparently dramatic transfer of sovereignty from national authorities to the international community. To this charge, there are three simple answers. First, it is the only way to achieve an effective adjustment process—without which the world economy will continue to suffer repeated crises with an ever-growing risk of serious breakdown. Second, the system is already evolving quite rapidly in this direction. The amount of the British devaluation of 1967 was, to a large extent, an internationally negotiated figure ; the amounts of the German revaluation and French devaluation of 1969 had been largely negotiated at the Bonn conference in late 1968 ; and the U.S. devaluation of 1971 was of course completely negotiated. The present proposal simply seeks to substitute timely negotiations based on internationally agreed criteria for these crisis-forced negotiations which involve a host of *ad hoc* judgments. Third, it has happened before. Robert Triffin's proposals for creating an international money were labelled utopian in the late 1950s for the same reasons, yet Special Drawing Rights were negotiated less than a decade later. Changes of similarly dramatic scope, again transferring apparent sovereignty from national to international hands, are needed in the adjustment arena now just as they were needed and then implemented in the liquidity arena in the past.

ELIMINATION OF THE PROBLEMS OF THE OVERHANG

Even with such new rules, however, effective adjustment in the future could be frustrated by a major legacy of the past—the dollar overhang. Conversions of outstanding dollar reserves into U.S. reserve assets, or even dollar shifts among foreign monetary authorities, could distort current payments patterns. Thus they could trigger undesirable exchange-rate changes, or prevent desirable changes, or both. Shifts of dollars between private and official hands could have the same effects. In the process, the overhang would continue to foster well-known confidence problems and jeopardize the aggregate level of world liquidity by posing an omnipresent threat to the existing level of U.S. reserves.

In addition, the United States should be able to add to its gross reserves when it runs surpluses in its basic balance of payments in the future. If the United States is to finance future *deficits* in its basic balance with reserve assets, which it should agree to do upon implementation of reforms along the lines proposed here, it will need larger reserves. Indeed, the U.S. ratio of reserves to imports is now below that of seven other members of the Group of Ten, and of most other industrialized countries.[2] Without disposition of the overhang, however, the United States could easily find itself financing its deficits by selling reserve assets and financing its surpluses by a rundown of foreign dollar holdings. Such a situation could obviously not persist for very long, even if the United States were in basic balance—or even surplus—over time. Indeed, a ten-year average of zero basic balance for the United States comprised of five years of $4 billion surpluses and five years of $4 billion deficits, financed in such a way, would virtually wipe out U.S. reserves even if SDRs were created at an annual rate of $4 billion throughout this period and allocated on the present basis of IMF quotas.

Elimination of the problems of the dollar overhang thus constitutes a second prerequisite to monetary reform from a U.S. standpoint. This can be done in at least three different ways : elimination of the entire overhang via mandatory conversion by all countries of all of their reserve (as opposed to working balance) dollars into SDRs (or a new international account) ; mandatory conversion for the Group of Ten countries, with no provisions for reserve dollars held by others ; or voluntary conversion for all countries combined with a clear understanding that any dollars retained in national reserves were forever inconvertible into U.S. assets.

The first approach is by far the neatest and most elegant. Nevertheless, it would require forcing all countries to convert all of their reserve

[2] See Annex 2 for details.

dollars, which might be unacceptable to many of them and hence jeopardize passage of the necessary amendments to the Articles of Agreement of the International Monetary Fund.

The second would presumably be easier to negotiate since it disregards dollar reserves held by countries outside the Group of Ten. This would, however, leave at least $10 to 15 billion outstanding, preserving that much of the dangers cited above. It might also leave unresolved the disposition of the dollars that later moved to the Group of Ten countries. Politically, it would create two sharply different classes of dollar holders by making a new option available only to some of the rich.

However, both national choice over reserve portfolio composition and equivalent treatment of all countries can be maintained, while eliminating the monetary problems of the overhang, through a two-part "optional consolidation". First, a special issue of SDRs could be authorized for conversion of all reserve assets (including sterling and gold, as well as dollars) outstanding at the time of the agreement. Following the lead of the Basel arrangements for sterling, the authorization should cover dollars and sterling held privately at that time as well ; they could otherwise move into official reserves and cause the problems outlined above, so they too should be eligible for consolidation into the special issue of SDRs if they move into official reserves and the authorities do not wish to hold onto them.

Second, countries could elect to retain some or all of their dollars or other assets, but these could be used in the future only to finance payments deficits—*à la* the SDR "needs test"—and would no longer be convertible into other assets via the key currency countries. (Countries would presumably keep working balances in dollars, which by definition would be used only to finance their payments deficits.) The United States would no longer automatically convert "old" dollars into gold, or gold into dollars. The option to convert into the special issue of SDRs could be exercised by a particular country either at once or in the future. It could be exercised by the country holding a particular asset at the time of the agreement, or by a country acquiring it later through the settlement of payments imbalances. The restrictions on the use of the dollars prior to conversion into the special issue of SDRs would render them harmless to the system and to the United States ; delayed conversion would thus be feasible. Whether the reserve dollars were retained or converted into the special issue of SDRs, they would be removed as a problem for the United States and for the monetary system as a whole.

The major drawback of this approach is its technical complexity, particularly since it would probably be linked with optional arrangements for "new" dollars acquired from future U.S. basic deficits. ("New" dollars could either be converted into U.S. reserve assets immediately, or retained in inconvertible form by countries which preferred to do so. They could, however, still be converted into U.S. assets if they subsequently shifted to countries which did not wish to hold them and so would not necessarily provide lasting financing for U.S. deficits.) The technical problems are nevertheless manageable and are simply part of the much closer international cooperation which must exist at all levels, from statistics to high policy, in the future. This is the only approach which deals comprehensively with the problems of the overhang while permitting countries to maintain sovereign control over the composition of their reserve assets.

Two specific aspects of any consolidation scheme are of particular importance to the United States : the disposition of the dollars converted into the special issue of SDRs and the interest-rate provisions. The dollars could be retained by the IMF and redeemed by the United States with its reserve assets, either on a fixed schedule or whenever it ran payments surpluses ; retained indefinitely by the IMF as interest-bearing "consols" ; or returned to the United States and eliminated altogether. In considering these issues, it must be remembered that the United States will undertake an obligation to guarantee the gold value of all SDRs created to consolidate outstanding dollars, in marked contrast to the present situation where very few dollar reserves even carry exchange-rate guarantees.

U.S. amortization of the overhang could have a severe deflationary effect on the world economy. It has already been noted that the United States will need to build its reserves. Any dollar repayment obligation would thus add to the magnitude of the payments surpluses targeted by the United States. Reconciliation of the essentially mercantilistic trade and payments objectives of most other nations has been very difficult in the past, with the United States playing an essentially passive and accommodating role ; it will become extremely difficult even with the United States aiming for small surpluses to build its reserves ; and it could become unmanageable if the United States aimed at sufficiently high surpluses to achieve the desired reserve growth *plus* pay off debt. It is quite possible that $30 billion will be consolidated, so that even a 50-year amortization schedule would add $600 million to the annual U.S. payments target. (The British surplus target might also have to rise by $100 million to pay off the $5 billion of sterling which could come in.)

In addition, there is no one to redeem any gold converted into the special issue of SDRs, so an amortization requirement for reserve currencies would require different treatment of the different assets now outstanding. It would also create "backing" for these SDRs (as would even IMF holding of U.S. "consols"), and hence raise questions and technical problems concerning the absence of "backing" for the regular SDRs.

Most important, the other countries will by definition be getting an asset which they prefer to the "old" dollars. There is thus no reason from their standpoint, or from the standpoint of the system, why the

United States should amortize. The only argument for amortization is that the United States should not "get away with" the past appropriation of real resources from the rest of the world accomplished through its payments deficits. The answer to this is that many of these dollar holdings were the result of foreign demand (for reserves and exports) rather than of U.S. supply, so others *wanted* the United States to take some of those resources ; that many of the dollars which *were* supply-generated resulted from expenditures in the global interest, ranging from the Marshall Plan through NATO ; and, most importantly, that the United States will assure against the re-creation of a new overhang by agreeing to finance its basic deficits in the future entirely with reserve assets.

The United States would thus strongly prefer the third approach—total retirement of the consolidated dollars—and has good grounds for doing so in terms of the interests of the system as well as of its more narrow national interests. Indeed, the United States might prefer to remain inconvertible, or to take its chances with the overhang at the risk of going inconvertible again, rather than to accept arrangements even as superficially generous as the 50-year repayment schedule mentioned above in addition to the gold-value guarantee attached to the specially created SDRs.

On the interest-rate issue, there are five basic approaches. The first is to treat the new SDRs as "initial allocations", on which no interest is paid. The second is for the United States to pay the IMF amounts sufficient only for it to pay interest to the holders of the new SDRs at the current SDR interest rate of 1 $1/2$ per cent, or some new (presumably higher) rate which would apply to all SDRs. The third is for the United States to pay the IMF amounts equal to the "normal" U.S. debt service burden on the consolidated dollars—this "normal" rate being equal to current U.S. market rates on the debt instruments which were originally consolidated, or to some "average" current U.S. interest rate, or to some average U.S. debt service level in the past, or simply to some negotiated rate agreeable to all—with this rate passed on to the holders of the special SDRs, and with lower rates continuing to apply to regular SDRs. The fourth is for the United States to continue its "normal" payments, with the present (or some other lower) rate prevailing for all SDRs, the difference being used to amortize the dollar "principal". The fifth is for some new use to be found for this difference.

All of these approaches are consistent with returning the consolidated dollars to the United States, as just proposed. The special issue of SDRs would be treated as a "net use" of SDRs by the United States and a "net acquisition" by other countries, with interest paid through book transfers as under the present SDR scheme. The Fund need not actually hold any dollar instruments.

Avoiding interest payments altogether on the new SDRs would of course maximize the financial savings to the United States, and be extremely attractive to it. However, there would be technical problems in treating these SDRs as "initial allocations" rather than as "net use" by the United States, and attempting to do so would intensify the opposition on moral grounds to the entire consolidation scheme.

The alternative of increasing the interest rate on all SDRs to equate it fully or at least more nearly with the interest rate on dollars has serious disadvantages. Countries will gain a gold-value guarantee by converting their dollars into SDRs and can hardly expect to receive an equally high interest rate as well. In addition, higher interest rates on "net acquisitions" of SDRs would make payments surpluses even more attractive than they are now, and payments deficits even costlier ; it would hence exacerbate the adjustment bias of the system against deficit countries, whereas a key objective of the needed adjustment reforms is to eliminate or at least reduce this bias. It is doubtful that such a proposal could even receive serious consideration in the IMF since enough countries probably anticipate deficit positions over time to block the amendment to the Articles of Agreement which would be necessary.

The alternative of paying a higher interest rate on the special issue of SDRs than on regular SDRs is also undesirable. It would actually require creation of a totally different asset, to avoid insuperable technical problems when the SDRs shift hands, and thus undermine rather than enhance the movement toward reliance on a single international asset for world liquidity.

The two viable choices are thus (*a*) U.S. payments to the Fund equal to the interest rate paid to SDR holders, at or near the present 1 1/2 per cent, or (*b*) higher U.S. payments based on some notion of a "fair" burden for the United States, with a decision as to how to use the difference. For reasons already outlined, there is no utility in using the difference to "redeem" the U.S. debt. The most promising method for using it, and the most likely to develop strong political support, is to seize this opportunity to forge a link between the SDR system and development finance. The difference could be granted to the World Bank to augment the lending capabilities of its International Development Association. Consolidation of $30 billion, with SDR rates remaining at 1 1/2 per cent and U.S. interest obligations set at 4 1/2 per cent, would generate $900 million annually for development. The "burden" of this aid would be shared by the previous holders of the dollars—who would give up their interest earnings in return for the gold-value guarantee and systemic effects of the SDRs—and the United States—which would actually be paying the interest and might otherwise have seen its interest burden reduced. Some of the lower income countries may have to be bribed to go along with an overall reform program such as is outlined here and this interest provision seems the best way to do so consistently with the basic monetary needs of the industrialized world.

ENOUGH RESERVE GROWTH

The third U.S. requirement for monetary reform is assured expansion of international liquidity at a pace sufficient to enable countries to achieve their own reserve-growth targets without taking reserves away from each other, and without relying on the dollar. Anything less would undermine two of the basic objectives of these over-all reforms : the elimination of the present asymmetrical pressure on deficit countries to take most of the adjustment initiatives and a reduction of the role of the dollar in the system.

In addition, such aggregate liquidity growth through non-dollar means is the only way for the United States to achieve its new objective of reserve increases. The United States would want liquidity growth to be even larger if it had to amortize the consolidated dollars—instead of their being retired, as proposed above—in order to avoid major new pressures on the world economy.

A number of studies, in addition to the actual decision on the first allocation of Special Drawing Rights, indicate that world reserves should rise by at least 5-6 per cent annually. At current rates of world inflation, this amounts to real growth of only 1-3 per cent, and suggests that even higher nominal growth may be necessary.

Such growth should be achieved wholly through creation of SDRs. The SDR creation will have to be larger than the desired increase in reserves, however, since 30 per cent of each country's SDR holdings must now be "reconstituted" within five years and hence represents medium-term credit rather than "owned reserves". (It would be preferable to abolish reconstitution altogether and to introduce several other changes in the SDR rules to improve the "moneyness" of the asset and further reduce the distinctions between it and other reserve assets.) New rules will also be needed to assure that increases in other reserve assets—mainly dollars but also gold, and sterling and other national currencies—do not throw total reserve growth off course as in 1970-1971.

The last reform concerns the need for new mechanisms to deal with the huge movements of liquid capital which will continue to pervade the system, despite their being dampened by the widening of exchange-rate margins. The United States has a particular interest in this aspect of reform because the vehicle currency role of the dollar assures that such movements will lead to dollar accruals to foreign monetary authorities whenever the flows are away from the United States. (The United States could not possibly be expected to finance such movements from its reserves, and the previous discussion of U.S. asset financing has therefore been confined to U.S. *basic* deficits.)

The liquid flows could be checked directly, but effective controls would have to cover a wide range of international transactions comprehensively and thus bear significant economic costs. The best remedy is to sharply expand the swap network to offset the effects of these flows on national reserves. The network should be greatly enlarged, perhaps to $50 billion from the present $11 billion for a starter, to credibly cover any possible level of flows. Maturities of swaps should be longer, perhaps 18-24 months relative to the present standard of 3-6 months, since it often takes that long to eliminate the interest-rate differentials which trigger the flows. And the swaps should carry full exchange-rate guarantees instead of the partial guarantees which exist at present.

CONCLUSION

With these four fundamental improvements in the monetary system, the United States should be willing to resume full convertibility of the dollar into U.S. reserve assets and all of its other international monetary obligations. It should also be willing to see the dollar continue to serve as a transaction and intervention currency for all who wish to use it—and even as a reserve asset for those who want it under the restricted conditions outlined. Most important, the United States should be willing to commit itself to finance all future deficits in its basic balance of payments with reserve assets. Without such reforms, the United States will be sorely tempted to try to preserve the pure dollar standard which has existed since 15 August 1971.

Fortunately, the same reforms are in the interest of other countries as well. At a minimum, they would bring the United States and the dollar back into the system. Beyond this, however, all countries would gain from improving the adjustment process, eliminating the problems of the dollar overhang, and assuring adequate international liquidity. It is hard to see how such goals could be accomplished except through greater flexibility of exchange rates and creation of enough Special Drawing Rights. Both of these steps would, moreover, accelerate the progress toward cooperative international management of the monetary system to replace the dollar hegemony and/or disorganized multipolar scrambles for power of the recent past. The bases for rapid progress toward reform thus appear to be present in the national interests of all countries, and the great need is to get on with it.

GUIDELINES FOR ECONOMIC ADJUSTMENT *

Economic situation	Open or closed economy	Demand policy	Selective policy	Exchange rate
(1) Full employment, rapid inflation, payments deficit (classic "non-dilemma" case)	Both	Restraint	(Manpower policy)	—
(2) Full employment, stable prices, payments deficit	Open Closed	Restraint —	Manpower policy (Incomes policy)	— Devaluation
(3) Full employment, rapid inflation, payments surplus (classic "dilemma" case)	Both	—	(Manpower policy)	Revaluation
(4) Full employment, stable prices, payments surplus	Open Closed	Expansion —	Manpower policy Manpower policy	Revaluation Revaluation
(5) Unemployment, rapid inflation, payments deficit	Open Closed	— Expansion	Incomes policy Incomes policy	Devaluation Devaluation
(6) Unemployment, stable prices, payments deficits (classic "dilemma" case)	Both	—	(Incomes policy)	Devaluation
(7) Unemployment, rapid inflation, payments surplus	Open Closed	Expansion —	Incomes policy (Manpower policy)	— Revaluation
(8) Unemployment, stable prices, payments surplus (classic "non-dilemma" case)	—	Expansion	(Incomes policy)	—

* Parentheses around a particular policy mean that the need for it is uncertain, and would depend on the circumstances of the particular country at the particular time.

Annex 2

RESERVE ADEQUACY OF GROUP OF TEN COUNTRIES

Country	Reserves (in millions of dollars)	Months of imports covered
(1) Switzerland	6,549	12.0
(2) Japan	14,100	8.7
(3) Germany	16,957	6.4
(4) Italy	6,666	5.1
(5) France	7,310	4.4
(6) Canada	5,072	4.0
(7) Belgium	3,424	3.4
(8) United States	12,130	3.2
(9) Netherlands	3,609	2.8
(10) United Kingdom	5,013	2.6
(11) Sweden	998	1.7

Data are for 30 September 1971 except for Japan and Canada, where they are for 31 October 1971.

Eurodollars, Reserve Dollars, and Asymmetries in the International Monetary System

4

Richard N. COOPER
Yale University

During the past decade economists and a growing number of others have become concerned with the possible instability of the gold-exchange standard. An international monetary system that satisfies a growing portion of its requirements for international reserves by relying on some national currency must eventually face the prospect that the national currency will cease to be convertible into other reserve assets, and this prospect will induce destabilizing shifts in the composition of reserves. In 1971 the prospect became a reality, when the United States abandoned its commitment to buy and sell gold freely, a move that was apparently in part prompted by the anxious attempts of several central banks to convert to gold or otherwise protect the value of their reserves in the face of large acquisitions of dollars.

The presence of this problem has led to a number of proposed solutions, most of which require the consolidation of reserve currency holdings, usually in exchange for some international asset (such as SDRs) at a suitably modified International Monetary Fund, thereby removing or greatly reducing the discretion central banks have over the composition of their reserves.

More recently, growing restlessness and even irritation at the special position of the reserve currencies, the U.S. dollar and to a less extent the pound sterling (as evidenced by the persistent presence of this issue in Britain's negotiations for entry into the European Economic Community), and the advantages that allegedly accrue therefrom to the United States and Britain—an "exorbitant privilege", as de Gaulle called it—have been added to concern over the instability of a system relying on national currencies for international reserves. The result has been a growing demand in the European press and public discussion for greater symmetry among national currencies, for putting on Britain and the United States the same financial burdens and responsibilities that fall on other countries with respect to their foreign payments.

Symmetry is quite a different issue from the problem of potential instability, but several of the proponents for consolidation of reserves have also echoed the sentiment for symmetry in burdens and responsibilities. These observers have been joined by others, mostly Americans, who seek greater symmetry largely to improve the capacity of the United States to adjust its balance-of-payments position, especially through changes in exchange rates—a perspective obviously very different from that of those Europeans who emphasize the privileges involved in having one's currency used widely abroad.

Thus the arguments in favor of consolidation of foreign-exchange reserves are : (1) that it will reduce an important source of instability in the system, (2) that it will eliminate the special privileges arising from the ability of the reserve currency countries, in effect, to print international money, and (3) that it will permit those countries to deal with imbalances in payments more readily through changes in exchange rates, without being concerned, as they now must be, with a whole range of inhibiting factors not present for other countries.

It is usually assumed in discussing the need for symmetry or for reserve consolidation that certain other central features of the present international payments will remain unchanged. In particular, reliance continues to be placed on private exchange markets for multilateral clearing of international payments, and on maintenance of official exchange-rate obligations by intervention in that market by central banks as buyers and sellers of their own currency against a single foreign currency, usually the U.S. dollar. It is also generally assumed that the vast growth in private international transactions and currency dealings has on balance been a healthy one, so that any changes in these private markets, including the Euro-currency market, should be relatively modest ones, in the interests only of ensuring against instability there. Some observers have expressed deeper concerns about the Euro-currency market, but wide differences of opinion, combined with general recognition of the real benefits to be derived from this market, augur against major changes without a major crisis clearly attributable to the market.

I contend that there is a contradiction between the desire for symmetry among currencies and the disposition to continue present clearing arrangements and the private use of national currencies (where by symmetry I mean inability to distinguish legally among any two national currencies in official arrangements) ; and in addition that the deep asymmetries in the international monetary system will create problems for reserve consolidation that have not yet been adequately explored.

This paper first draws attention to the fundamental asymmetries in the world financial system, to the reasons for them, and to their implications for official monetary arrangements ; it then sketches the radical changes that will be necessary in order to achieve symmetry, draws attention to some of the difficulties created for reserve consolidation by the asymmetries, and offers some possible resolutions to these difficulties.

I. ASYMMETRIES IN THE WORLD FINANCIAL SYSTEM

The basic asymmetry of course is the dominant economic size of the United States, reinforced by the closely related asymmetries in scale and sophistication of financial markets. These are subject to secular change, but only gradually and over rather long periods of time. These asymmetries in turn lead through a complicated process that will not concern us here to two separate but related asymmetries in the operation of international payments : the extensive private use of the U.S. dollar as a medium of exchange, a unit of account, and a temporary store of value, and use of the dollar as an official intervention currency in a payments system that relies on private markets for multilateral clearing, as the Bretton Woods system in practice does.

Reasons for the Asymmetries

The reasons for these asymmetries are deep-seated, residing in the enormous efficiency of money as an intermediary in the process of exchange. Classical monetary theory recognized the social value of money without being clear about its sources and without integrating money into the theory of exchange. Recent work on these aspects of the theory of money has begun to explore more precisely what is the role of money in exchange, and why some medium of exchange will emerge out of a barter economy.[1] Barter trade suffers from the rarity of a "double coincidence" and the difficulty of carrying on multilateral trade. Under barter, a man with commodity A who wants commodity B must find a trading partner who has commodity B and wants commodity A ; or he must find someone who has C and wants A and then someone who has B and wants C, etc. Any trade incurs search costs—the variable costs associated with finding the relevant trading partners ; transfer costs—the

[1] See especially Jürg Niehans, "Money in a Static Theory of Optimal Payments Arrangements", *Journal of Money, Credit, and Banking,* Vol. 1 (November, 1969) ; pp. 702-26 ; *idem,* "Money and Barter in General Equilibrium with Transactions Costs", and Karl Brunner and Allan H. Meltzer, "The Uses of Money : Money in the Theory of an Exchange Economy", both in *American Economic Review,* Vol. 61 (December 1971) ; pp. 773-783 and 784-805, respectively ; and Morris Perlman, "The Roles of Money in an Open Economy and the Optimum Quantity of Money", *Economica,* Vol. 38 (August 1971) ; pp. 233-252.

costs (*e.g.* transportation) associated with making the physical exchange; and storage costs—the interest foregone and actual losses through theft and spoilage involved while the search and transfer process is going on. There are obviously some trade-offs among these costs, but their totality can be reduced greatly by the institution not only of trading posts, which bring would-be traders together at agreed times and places, but also of a common medium of exchange which by facilitating multilateral trade eliminates the need for a double coincidence.

Qualitatively the problems of a barter economy arise in the international markets for national monies, with the monies taking the place of commodities: the problem is now to facilitate multilateral clearing and avoid the need for double coincidences.[2] The costs of search for double coincidences rise sharply with the number and diversity of participants; with over 100 currencies representing an equal number of very diverse economies the economic advantages of multilateral exchange are considerable. Thus it becomes efficient to have an international medium of exchange, reducing the number of currency markets from over 5000 to around 100 (from n(n-1)/2 to n-1, where n is the number of currencies). It is quite natural, although not necessary, that this common medium should be the currency of the largest trading nation, for that will reduce both search and transfer costs. Moreover, a medium of exchange is likely to seek a temporary store of value of the same denomination, for that will reduce total transactions costs further and will also reduce the uncertainty arising from a fluctuating price between the store of value and the units of account of trading contracts, which are efficiently the same as those of the medium of exchange. And once it becomes a store of value, the importance of large and efficient (low cost) financial markets is reinforced.

All of this amounts to what we already know: that the world's "public" will find it convenient to hold and use some common medium of exchange for international transactions, formerly silver and gold, then sterling and the dollar. The reasons are deep-seated, not superficial, for these arise from the major economies in making international payments. Any tendency to attribute this process to Eurodollars mistakes the symptom for the cause. U.S. liquid liabilities to private foreigners were $15 billion in December 1971 (some to be sure representing inter-bank liabilities to the Eurodollar market), but they were $7 billion even in 1960, when the Eurodollar market was in its infancy and world trade was

[2] This point has also been made by Alexander K. Swoboda, *The Eurodollar Market: An Interpretation,* Essays in International Finance, No. 64, Princeton, International Finance Section, February 1968; pp. 5-10, and "Vehicle Currencies and the Foreign Exchange Market: The Case of the Dollar", in Robert Z. Aliber (ed.), *The International Market for Foreign Exchange,* Praeger, 1969; pp. 30-40.

only about one-third of that reached in 1971. Furthermore, the reasons adduced above for private foreign dollar holding suggest that these dollars are not merely the unwanted residue of past U.S. payments deficits ; on the contrary, the foreign demand for dollars in the sixties may have been one of the *causes* of the deficits, defined in the pre-1971 fashion on the liquidity basis, and may thus have helped to frustrate various American attempts to reduce the deficit.

All of this concerns private markets. Under a system of exchange-rate parities, the responsibility falls on central banks to act as residual buyers or sellers of their currency of issue. The home currency must be traded against something, and it is not only entirely natural but generally most efficient to use the medium most readily accepted in the private community. One can easily conceive of the use of other currencies for intervention, with reliance on the efficiency of the private market for arbitrage against all other currencies. The difficulty lies in the possible need for rapid mobilization and use of large amounts of the medium for intervention purposes ; unless the economy whose currency is used is a large one, large-scale use of its currency may play havoc with its domestic monetary conditions ; and conversion into cash of balances held temporarily in interest-bearing securities can depress security prices, thereby imposing losses on the holder, if large amounts are sold suddenly. Both difficulties could of course be overcome with the proper international institutional arrangements, but until the advent of the EEC's plans for monetary unification there has seemed no compelling reason to find a substitute for the dollar as a currency of intervention.

Results of the Asymmetries

Use of the dollar as an official intervention currency and private international use of the dollar in turn have several asymmetrical effects on the actual functioning of the international payments system and on balance-of-payments adjustment through changes in exchange rates. Use of the dollar as an intervention currency limits the maximum movement in market exchange rates between the dollar and any other currency to one-half what it is between any other pair of currencies, for the simple reason that direct intervention controls possible movement vis-a-vis the dollar, whereas market arbitrage is relied upon to provide limits between other trades.[3] This in turn limits the relative price adjustment that can take

[3] The maximum swing can be even wider between a currency whose authorities use the dollar and a currency whose authorities use the pound sterling as an intervention currency.

place through exchange-rate changes between the United States and other countries, compared with other pairs of countries, in the absence of changes in parities, and thereby impedes adjustment in some circumstances.

Second, the use of the dollar as an intervention currency in practice entails at least working balances to be held in dollars, and the dollar thus also takes on the status of a reserve currency.

Third, the use of the dollar as an intervention currency greatly complicates taking the *initiative* for changes of the parity of the dollar. Detailed advance consultation is difficult because of the likelihood of "leaks" and the resulting speculation ; while without such consultation, officials of other countries must decide, following announcement of a change in dollar parity, without opportunity to analyze the change in question, whether to alter their intervention points or not, knowing that they will be held responsible to their publics for any "initiative" one way or the other. This uncertainty concerning how others will respond in turn has led American authorities to consider a change in parity less favorably than they otherwise might have. An alteration of the adjustment process in favor of smaller and more frequent changes in exchange rates should mitigate this problem by reducing the amount at stake in any single change in parity.

The extensive private international use of the dollar also has several implications for the international payments system. First, it means that other countries can be running dollar surpluses when the United States is not running a deficit or, to put it more accurately (since that depends on the choice of definition of deficit and surplus), other nations may be calling on the United States to convert large amounts of dollars into other reserve assets even when residents of the United States are not engaging in net spending abroad, or even (conceivably) when they are selling more goods, services, and securities to non-residents than they are buying from non-residents.

Second, private international use of the dollar greatly complicates the *capacity* of the United States to achieve a change in parity against other currencies. Extensive valuation of trading contracts and assets abroad in dollars means that a change in its parity would generate bankruptcy or lesser complications for otherwise viable banks and firms. Thus when the pound sterling was devalued in 1967, Hong Kong and Jamaica both also devalued at once, although the payments position of neither area warranted it. Hong Kong banks with assets in sterling and liabilities in Hong Kong dollars could have been bankrupt by a large change in the rate between the two. Four days later Hong Kong solved this problem by indemnifying the banks out of official reserves, and revalued the Hong Kong dollar part way. Jamaica had outstanding sugar and banana export contracts in sterling, revenues against a wage bill in Jamaican currency. Devaluation of the pound against the Jamaican dollar would have bankrupt the firms, so Jamaica followed sterling down. It is unclear how Japan handled a similar problem with its ship-building and other industries following the December 1971 revaluation of the yen against the U.S. dollar. But Japan's two-week delay in allowing the value of the yen to rise, during which time the Bank of Japan took in several billion dollars from Japanese residents and banks, suggests the operation of a process of prior indemnification out of official reserves.

II. HOW CAN SYMMETRY BE ACHIEVED?

Following this exploration of the existing asymmetries between the reserve currencies and other currencies, we can return to the question posed at the outset, and ask whether it is possible to achieve legal symmetry among currencies while still retaining existing private markets and market clearing practices. The answer, it will now be clear, is that it is not possible ; more far-reaching changes would be required to achieve symmetry, involving a new non-national private international currency or at least a clearing union. Before turning to those possibilities it will be useful to dwell on some of the difficulties of introducing symmetry, for these difficulties also bear on the more limited objective of consolidating reserve currency assets.

First, as noted above, use of an intervention currency introduces an asymmetry in exchange-rate movements between the intervention limits. The Bretton Woods Agreement is written with symmetrical requirements for all currencies, but these had to be abandoned in view of intervention practices ; as a result, many pairs of currencies have traded at rates outside the two per cent band-width around the ratios of their parities, despite the formal requirement to avoid this.[4] The Werner Committee on Monetary Unification in the European Community also had to wrestle with this problem in its attempt to narrow exchange rate movements among European currencies without narrowing them with respect to the dollar—while still retaining the dollar as an intervention currency. They produced a solution that is technically feasible but cumbersome ; it involved the close coordination of market intervention by member countries to narrow the band of exchange-rate variation vis-à-vis the dollar on any

---

[4] Art. IV, Sec. 2 of the IMF Articles of Agreement stipulates that all spot currency transactions within a member country's territory shall be kept within one per cent of parity—a band-width of two per cent. An IMF decision in 1959 doubled this limit to allow for intervention in dollars (or indeed in any other convertible currency). This decision was superseded by the decision of December 1971 to widen the band-width to 4 $^{1}/_{2}$ per cent against the intervention currency, hence as much as 9 per cent between any other pair of currencies.

given day, but to vary the mid-point of that band from week to week, allowing it in principle to vary over the whole range permitted by a given set of parities (dubbed by wags "a snake in a tunnel"). But on any given day the maximum variation of the dollar with respect to any currency is still only half what it is for any other pair of currencies, and in addition some member countries would be denied desirable variation with respect to the dollar by the requirement to coordinate with other members. Why did the Werner Committee not recommend a European intervention currency which would have greatly simplified achievement of their immediate objective? The answer was no doubt partly the inability to agree on one, but more basically it was rooted in the considerations mentioned in the preceding section, namely the technical advantage in dealing in a currency whose market for other currencies was sufficiently broad that active intervention would influence the market without disrupting it, and the parallel advantage of being able to invest temporarily excess holdings of the intervention currency in interest-yielding assets whose price would not be unduly influenced by movements into and out of cash.[5]

Second, suppose the reserve currency role of the dollar is eliminated by requiring (unrealistically, in view of the need for working balances, taken up below) all reserve assets to be held in some common, nationally neutral form, such as SDRs. Dollars taken up through exchange market intervention must be converted into such assets immediately, and dollars needed for intervention would be acquired through instantaneous conversion of SDRs. What shall be the rate of exchange between dollars and SDRs? Between other currencies and SDRs? One's first inclination is to say that each currency will trade against SDRs at its par value. But if the market rates among currencies differ from par value relationships, trading SDRs against currencies at par would create the possibility of profitable arbitrage, with the attractions being all the greater now that the permissable band width has been widened from 2 to 4 1/2 per cent. To avoid this, the dollar must trade against SDRs at parity, but other currencies must trade against SDRs at rates influenced by the market rate

[5] After the currency disruptions of late 1971, the European Community agreed that each member of the community accomplish this objective, not by coordinating their market intervention in dollars as under the Werner Plan, but by intervening in the currencies of *each* other member country as needed. Intervention in dollars would be confined to the vicinity of the borders of the new 4 1/2 per cent band of flexibility, while exchange-rate variations among member currencies are to be held to the same range by direct intervention, rather than to twice that range as would result from exclusive use of the dollar as an intervention currency. This move not only underestimated the need for greater flexibility, as was illustrated by the floating of the British pound barely a month after the plan started, but also underestimated the difficulty of simultaneous intervention in several currencies whenever a central bank wants to intervene *within* the permissible limits.

against the dollar.[6] Thus the dollar would be legally distinguishable from other currencies.

Alternative arrangements are possible, avoiding this need for asymmetry, but they involve costs. For instance, a charge could be levied for conversions into and out of SDRs sufficiently large to discourage conversions for arbitrage gains. On its normal operations, in which currencies do exchange at par, the IMF levies a service charge of 1/2 per cent that partially performs this function. But 1/2 per cent would not be large enough to eliminate arbitrage when exchange margins are as large as 2 1/4 per cent on each side of parity, and in any case it would represent a compulsory tax on *all* reserve transactions under the circumstances hypothesized above, a charge that would unduly discourage the use of reserves.[7] A second alternative would stipulate that each country deal against SDRs (at par) in only *one* national currency (any one) other than its own, and could not change its choice of currency except under international supervision ; but under this requirement most countries would choose the U.S. dollar, again preserving *de facto* asymmetry.

Third, in practice use of an intervention currency entails the holding of working balances, so that the monetary authorities are able if necessary to intervene quickly to prevent unwanted movements in exchange rates. But once working balances are allowed, the reserve currency role has again made its appearance. Unless they are subjected to some limit, these working balances are likely to give rise to all the problems of a gold-exchange standard, noted briefly at the outset. Under a market clearing system, the *sources* of dollar accruals to a central bank are not immediately known, and in some cases they may never be known accurately.[8]

---

[6] Strictly speaking, what is required is that the *structure* of market rates among currencies be maintained in dealings against SDRs ; *any* currency could be chosen to trade against SDRs at par, or indeed at any other fixed value ; but unless the dollar were chosen for this role arbitrary reserve losses or gains would result from turnaround transactions—selling reserves for intervention dollars and then replenishing them when the market rate between the dollar and the designated currency had changed. In any case asymmetry would result—the point the next tries to establish.

[7] The IMF service charge was one of the stumbling blocks to making the gold tranche into a fully usable reserve asset, and since the IMF amendments of 1969 the service charge has been dropped on gold tranche drawings, which still take place at par, with no observation of arbitrage to date. In its dealings in SDRs, however, the IMF follows the practice outlined above, fixing the price at parity in terms of the U.S. dollar, with transactions against other currencies taking place at market rates.

[8] More rapid and more accurate reporting from the Eurodollar market will help in this identification, but it will not entirely solve the problem because of the possibilities for credit expansion or contraction in the Eurodollar market. Thus a recorded decline in Eurodollar balances, for example, does not necessarily indicate an equivalent shift of funds either to the United States or into other currencies.

Thus if the inflows are exceptionally large, the initial presumption must be that they are short-term funds, in principle reversible, and to avoid transactions costs on the turn-around the central bank may reasonably decide to accumulate the dollars it purchases. But once dollars have accumulated, and the inflows are discovered to be non-reversible, it may be awkward (*e.g.* threaten the system) to convert them into other reserve assets. Moreover, genuine ambiguities over the reversible character of the accruals will permit subtle pressure by the United States not to convert, thereby retaining one of the features of the gold/SDR exchange standard that some observers find most objectionable.

Alternatively, fixing some limit to the magnitude of working balances (*e.g.* to 15 per cent of total reserves as in Triffin's proposal [9]) could also create difficulties for the United States because of the large outstanding private dollar balances and the possibility that they may be shifted into other currencies even when on other counts the U.S. payments position is in balance. These private funds, in the form of demand deposits, short-term time deposits, and marketable U.S. government securities, reached astounding proportions by late 1971 : $15 billion in liabilities of U.S. banks, another $30 billion in liabilities of their overseas branches, and an estimated $20 billion in the dollar liabilities of non-U.S. banks in the Eurodollar market. More will be said about them below. But the point here is that the United States does not have enough reserves to cover conversions into other currencies of even 20 per cent of these balances. Large-scale conversions would therefore lead the United States to break out of any system imposing convertibility, unless special provisions were made for this contingency, for example through large and virtually automatic lines of credit such as expansible "working balances" of reserve dollars automatically provide. But once again an asymmetry is recognized and a "special privilege" established, unless such lines of virtually automatic credit are also made available (in amounts proportional to some measure of economic size and requirements, *e.g.* to IMF quotas) to all member countries.

A Neutral International Money

Enough has been said above to support the view that use of an intervention currency is not consistent with complete symmetry among currencies, even leaving aside the asymmetry with respect to movements in

---

[9] Robert Triffin, "How to Arrest a Threatening Relapse into the 1930s", *Bulletin of the National Bank of Belgium* (November 1971).

exchange rates. A move to freely floating exchange rates would of course establish symmetry in official use of currencies ; but it might increase rather than diminish private international use of major national currencies, especially the dollar. Within the realm of fixed parities, a radical solution to this problem would abandon the use of a national currency for intervention purposes and, ultimately, for private market purposes. In the past the monetary metals served as neutral international monetary media ; Rueff's proposal for a major increase in the price of gold, the U.S. proceeds of which to be used to retire outstanding dollar balances, would have restored this neutrality if at the same time countries also maintained their currencies' parities by buying and selling gold rather than dollars. A forward-looking arrangement would place this role on a new international currency, a revised SDR, which would be used by national monetary authorities to maintain their market exchange rates within stipulated limits as well as held as reserves. Market intervention in SDRs would eliminate the first two asymmetries mentioned above —the narrower range of fluctuation in exchange rates with respect to the dollar, and the need to trade the dollar against SDRs at par, while not being able to do that for other currencies—but would of course require the development of private markets in SDRs, including SDR-denominated demand accounts and interest-bearing securities.[10] Gradually the third asymmetry then might also disappear, as international private holdings of dollars diminished to non-threatening proportions through the United States "earning" them back. But in fact it is difficult to contemplate such a substitution in private use of SDRs for dollars without major incentives to use SDRs and disincentives to the use of dollars. Run-away inflation in the United States soon after private SDRs are launched might for example accomplish the substitution. Even then the mantle might more readily pass to another national currency, or to a new European currency, if it then exists. It is difficult, moreover, to contemplate the successful introduction of an acceptable international currency for private use that does not also threaten the existence of national currencies in all but the largest countries, leading ultimately to a world currency.

[10] The medium of payment and store of value functions must here be distinguished. In particular, SDRs themselves need not bear interest in order to function effectively as an international medium of exchange—indeed, interest yield might even impair this function by encouraging at the margin deficit-reducing actions, which use social resources, rather than deficit-financing, which does not use social resources ; but there must be SDR-denominated interest-bearing assets if SDRs are to function fully as a private international currency.

Another, more limited, solution to the problem of asymmetries intrinsic in the use of a national currency for international purposes, but one still beyond current thinking about monetary reform, lies in abandonment of the foreign-exchange market for multilateral clearing, thus eliminating the need for market intervention, and establishment in its stead of an International Clearing Union. The Clearing Union would declare consistent fixed buying and selling rates for all pairs of currencies, so that when, for example, a German resident wanted to buy Turkish lire, a German commercial bank would provide the lire against German marks at a fixed rate, drawing the lire from the Bundesbank which in turn would draw them from the Clearing Union. At the end of the day all accounts would be cleared, with Germany's account at the Union being debited and Turkey's account being credited as a result of the above transaction. This approximates the way in which the Federal Reserve System works with respect to its twelve regional banks ; the European Payments Union also operated roughly on this basis, with the important difference that accounts were settled only every 30 days and beyond that period special credits were advanced. An International Clearing Union need not involve such granting of credit, although it might do so.

Any substantial difference between buying and selling rates would give rise to private foreign-exchange markets with rates fluctuating between the buying and selling rates, but central banks would be proscribed from intervening in those markets, for that would raise once again the need for an intervention currency.

Establishment of a Clearing Union would not displace the use of dollars in private markets, nor would it deal directly with the possibility of large scale conversions of these dollar balances into other currencies which would threaten the ability of the United States to maintain convertibility of the dollar into the international reserve asset (here, claims on the Clearing Union). But the Clearing Union itself might be empowered to act as a lender of last resort on such occasions and to provide credit in ample quantity and on reasonable terms. As noted above, such an arrangement would either have to recognize the special problem faced by the United States (and to a less extent by the United Kingdom), thereby acknowledging the asymmetry : or it would have to be made available to all, thereby resulting in a general transformation of the present system of conditional credits to one of (virtually) unconditional ones, except for time limits.

Moreover, a Clearing Union on these lines would result in a narrowing of the range within which market exchange rates can fluctuate around parities, in opposition to contemporary sentiment for widening the band, and would thus result in the need for closer harmonization of national monetary policies to avoid large movements of yield-sensitive funds between nations.

III. CONSOLIDATION OF RESERVE CURRENCY BALANCES

Full consideration of complete symmetry among currencies requires further discussion, but the observations in the preceding section suggest that it will require changes in the international monetary system far more extensive than those so far contemplated. The question remains : to what extent can official dollar balances be consolidated without complication arising from the asymmetries arising from the private and intervention uses of the dollar ? The answer, it seems to me, is that this separation is possible insofar as the objective is to reduce considerably a possible source of instability in the gold-exchange standard,[11] but that a "price" must be paid for this gain in formalization of several of the asymmetries that in fact exist. Several of these have already been touched on : the differential exchange margin, the differential treatment on conversion into reserve assets, and the need for special credit provisions arising from private use of the dollar.

---

[11] It should be observed that introduction of a system of gliding parities—or indeed any form of frequent change in parity—in which the parity of the dollar is also expected to change, as desired both by those interested in better adjustment and by those concerned with the "inequity" of a system in which the United States does not have to bear the alleged "burden" of initiating parity changes, makes more urgent but also more difficult the task of consolidating reserve currency assets. The task is more urgent because regular movements in the parity of the dollar (and sterling) would encourage shifts in the composition of reserves, into or out of dollars (and sterling). The task is more difficult because it raises the question who carries the exchange risk. For example, if the IMF exchanges a special issue of SDRs for official dollar balances, and then the dollar parity changes, would the United States indemnify the IMF for its loss in SDR-value under a depreciating dollar, or would the IMF carry this loss itself, by building a reserve out of interest earnings on the dollar balances ? Since market interest rates would reflect expectations regarding prospective depreciation, the IMF should carry the exchange risk if it earned market interest rates. But to some observers this would appear to be a highly inequitable asymmetry favoring the United States.

This problem could of course be avoided if the parity of the dollar did *not* change under a gliding parity system. But such a special status would not only appear highly inequitable to many observers (see, *e.g.* John Williamson, *The Choice of a Pivot for Parities,* Essays in International Finance, No. 90, Princeton, International Finance Section, November 1971 ; pp. 13-14), but might also limit somewhat the effective exchange rate adjustment for the United States, because of threshold effects under any operative gliding parity system. On the last point, see E. Howle and C. Moore, "Richard Cooper's Gliding Parity : A Proposed Modification" and my reply in the *Journal of International Economics,* Vol. 1 (November 1971) ; pp. 429-436 and pp. 437-442, respectively.

Acceptance of these asymmetries may be taken as concessions to the efficiency of a market clearing system based on the currency of the preponderant economic and financial area in a world that otherwise maintains, by and large, formal legal equality among nations. But two other, related, costs are associated with consolidation of dollar balances, one concerning official use of efficient markets and the other concerning the elasticity of global reserve growth. Finally, before the United States can accept full convertibility implied by such consolidation, special credit provisions will also have to be made with respect to private dollar holdings.

Denying Access to Financial Markets

To achieve their purposes over time, consolidation proposals cannot be confined to funding existing dollar balances, but must also deny the possibility for central banks to acquire dollar balances in the future (beyond those required for working balances). In other words, they must deny central banks access to highly efficient money and short-term securities markets outside their own countries. Thus consolidation of dollar balances will lead to some loss in efficiency by reducing reliance on market facilities, and these costs may fall disproportionately on smaller nations. It has been noted, in discussions of direct foreign investment, that the output of General Motors exceeds that of the majority of countries. Similarly, the liquid balances of Exxon Corp. exceed the official liquid balances of over two-thirds of the members of the IMF. Should these countries, which from a world-wide financial perspective are in some respects like medium-sized international firms, be denied the access to efficient financial markets that firms enjoy? This denial presumably involves a considerable efficiency loss, although as noted in the first section we do not know yet how to measure it.

The loss as it will appear to central banks, however, has a number of concrete and identifiable aspects. First, use of the market permits quick and anonymous movement of funds at low transactions costs, a feature that could be reproduced by the IMF, but only without a service charge and thus with the built-in asymmetrical treatment of the dollar noted above. Second, the market provides a source of short-term credit that (given the stickiness of quoted interest rates) often involves maintenance of "compensating balances" with the commercial bank from which the loan was obtained, balances that would be ruled out under the obligatory consolidation proposals. This difficulty could be eliminated by putting a nation's reserves on a net rather than a gross basis for the purpose of calculating allowable dollar balances, although such a practice, by making the true condition of the borrowing country more visible, would reduce some of the present advantages of borrowing reserves to dress up the balance sheet. Third, loans are often obtained by pledging owned reserves as collateral, and it is not clear that commercial banks would accept as collateral claims on the IMF (such as SDRs) that they cannot themselves own (just as they do not lend against real estate that cannot legally be transferred to them) ; but this problem could presumably be resolved too, if the IMF were willing to facilitate the resolution by interpreting the "balance-of-payments" requirement for SDRs to include making good on outstanding loans and then to underwrite the loan at the time it was made.

Elasticity of Supply of International Reserves

A second loss from consolidation of reserve assets arises from the resulting loss in elasticity to reserve creation. The IMF is finding it difficult to develop persuasive criteria for the amounts of SDRs to be created. Suppose that, despite their best efforts, the authorities guess wrong on the amounts required. If they err on the high side, international spending, especially by developing countries, will increase ; the result would be a higher money level of international transactions (reflecting some combination of real and nominal increases), on one hand, and augmentation of the reserves of those countries (which can be called reserve sinks) that do not respond to modestly higher reserve levels, for example because they pursue active and successful policies of domestic economic stabilization, on the other hand. If the IMF authorities err on the low side, international transactions will contract (below what they would otherwise be), probably through the greater use of restrictive controls, or through a larger-than-normal number of currency devaluations which will raise the national currency value of reserves, these two processes mitigated to the extent that reserves of "reserve sinks" can be drawn down and distributed to the rest of the world. (But the role of reserve sink is likely to be asymmetric, with large countries showing more response to reserve reductions than to reserve increases.)

Official use of the dollar as a reserve currency provides a relatively elastic supply of new reserves to compensate for any shortfall in global reserve creation far faster than could be made good through a sequence of currency devaluations, which in any case experience suggests are likely to be preceded and accompanied by controls and other restraints on international transactions.[12] Thus unless the adjustment process is improved very substantially, this elastic source of reserves, supplied through U.S.

[12] In the past decade restraints on imports preceded the devaluations by Canada, Britain, France, and the United States, not to mention large numbers of developing countries.

payments deficits induced by the shortage of reserves, could help avoid damage to the international economy brought about by restrictive national action.[13]

The loss of this elasticity must of course be weighed against the gains from breaking the link between reserve creation and independent developments in the U.S. payments position, a link that has in recent years introduced capricious changes in international reserves.

It might be noted in passing that both of these costs—the efficiency losses arising from proscribing central bank use of much of the market mechanism and the loss in elasticity of reserve supply to satisfy reserve needs—could be avoided if the consolidation of dollar reserve holdings were made once for all, so that the instability threatened by large existing dollar balances would be removed without limiting the accumulation of future balances. Such a "solution" would not of course solve the problem of stability among reserve assets for all time, for uncomfortably large dollar balances would perhaps accumulate in the future and the consolidation would then have to be repeated ; and it would not go even part way toward reducing the other asymmetries that some observers find objectionable. The costs of consolidation would be lower, but so would the benefits.

Elasticity of Supply of Official Credit

Finally, we return to the question of the private dollar balances. Presumably in exchange for consolidation of outstanding official dollar balances the United States will be expected to restore full convertibility of future dollar holdings into other reserve assets. But should the United States resume convertibility without some arrangement also covering the contingency of conversion of private dollar balances ? And can it be reasonably expected to, except possibly on the implicit understanding that if the contingency of large conversions did arise, the United States would cease to honor that obligation ? It should be noted that it was speculative

[13] Ronald McKinnon has emphasized this role of dollar reserves, and the efficiency of the mechanism whereby they are supplied, in his *Private and Official International Money : The Case for the Dollar,* Essays in International Finance, No. 74, Princeton, International Finance Section, April 1969 ; pp. 15-16. John Williamson has argued that the desired elasticity could be introduced by supplementary creations of SDRs keyed to the observed frequency and amount of currency devaluations. This scheme presupposes both an efficient adjustment mechanism (so that devaluation is used instead of controls or unwarranted domestic deflation) and that countries are free to devalue when they choose, even when they show a payments surplus, if in their view they are gaining insufficient reserves. See his *The Choice of a Pivot for Parities,* Essays in International Finance, No. 90, Princeton, International Finance Section, November 1971 ; p. 19.

movements in the *private* holdings of sterling, not the official holdings, that gave Britain trouble over the years ; and that private foreign dollar balances have gyrated substantially in recent years—to be sure, in response to changes in monetary policy in the United States and other countries—increasing by only $1.7 billion in 1968 but by a startling $8.7 billion in 1969, and then dropping by $6.5 billion in 1970 and by a further $7.4 billion in 1971.

It is of course also true that *American*-owned dollar balances can shift massively abroad on a scale never before imagined, and these are much larger than foreign-owned balances. This is one aspect of the growing interdependence among nations, and reinforces the point. But the key difference between these funds and foreign-owned balances is that if necessary the former can be more readily restrained by instructions to American banks, as Britain controlled outflows of resident capital years ago. Distinctions between resident and non-resident capital are of long-standing. But the Eurodollar market introduces two new elements into the picture : first, the United States could not fully control non-resident capital even if it desired to, for the institutions involved are beyond the jurisdictional reach of the United States ; and, second, the presence of non-resident *institutions* dealing in dollars also makes it much more difficult to control the flow of resident capital.

Nonetheless, the problem of massive conversion of Eurodollars into other currencies can also be exaggerated. Precisely because the Eurodollar market to some extent leads a separate existence from the United States, conversions out of Eurodollars introduce a corrective rise in Eurodollar interest rates, thereby increasing foreign private willingness to hold dollar claims ; but if this rise in interest rates induces yield-sensitive outflows from the United States, straining whatever controls the United States may have imposed, the conversions may become very much larger.

The problem of large conversions of private dollars into other currencies could be handled, in the context of reserve consolidation, by permitting the IMF to extend credit *automatically* to the United States to cover large hot-money flows (even those that can be attributed to U.S. monetary policy), in effect providing a gold tranche on a much larger scale. If the conversions out of dollars are short-lived, as they should be if the convenience of holding dollars is as great as I have portrayed it above, then this credit will be reversed automatically. This principle underlies the present network of swap arrangements, which serve a similar purpose. If the conversions are not short-lived, the United States would have a repayment obligation spread over a period of years. If that in turn led to a loss of reserves, depreciation of the dollar would be in order, and should be permitted by other countries.

It comes down to this : either the United States is put on a short tether, like other countries, or it is not. If the tether imposed by con-

The Role of a Developing European Monetary Union in a Reformed World Monetary System 5

Robert TRIFFIN
Yale University

I. INTRODUCTION

The agreement painfully hatched on 18 December by the Group of Ten was hailed by President Nixon as "the most significant monetary agreement in the history of the world". I would hardly go that far in describing an agreement that merely sets up a new—and undoubtedly more realistic—pattern of exchange rates, but that leaves unsolved all the basic questions arising from the utter collapse—on 15 August—of the international monetary system, after ten years of mounting crises and patchwork salvage operations.

The official communiqué itself candidly enumerates the awesome list of issues that remain to be negotiated in Phase II of the marathon discussions envisaged for the "reform of the international monetary system" :

(1) the appropriate means and divisions of responsibilities for defending stable exchange rates and for insuring a proper degree of convertibility of the system ;
(2) the proper role of gold, of reserve currencies, and of special drawing rights in the operation of the system ;
(3) the appropriate volume of liquidity ;
(4) the re-examination of the permissible margins of fluctuation around established exchange rates and other means of establishing a suitable degree of flexibility ;
(5) other measures dealing with movements of liquid capital.

As you know, I have spent the last fifteen years developing and disseminating my own answers to all these questions, and others, beginning with my book on *Europe and the Money Muddle,*[1] and ending—provi-

[1] Robert Triffin, *Europe and the Money Muddle,* New Haven, Yale University Press, 1957.

sionally—with my most recent article on "How to Arrest a Threatening Relapse into the 1930's ?" (in the November 1971 *Bulletin of the National Bank of Belgium).* This is not the place to rehash these previous contributions, especially as you will have benefited from far better advice at our morning session of today. Yet, they cannot fail to crop up in my discussion of "The Role of a Developing European Monetary Union in a Reformed World Monetary System", since this role will obviously depend on how a world system now in utter shambles will actually be put together again.

I shall proceed in two steps, discussing first what the European Community can and should do until world reforms are agreed upon, and secondly how a developing European Monetary Union should fit into such a new worldwide monetary system.

II. IMMEDIATE STEPS PENDING WORLDWIDE AGREEMENT

The immediate steps to be taken by the European Community, in cooperation with its prospective new members and other European countries, consist essentially in implementing as rapidly as possible the program outlined in the Werner Plan, and in accelerating the time-table initially envisaged for such implementation.

The need for such acceleration derives essentially from two new factors inserted into the data of the problem by the decisions of 15 August and of 18 December 1971.

The first is the temporary inconvertibility of the dollar, not only into gold, but in any other international assets or currencies as well. This creates a gaping void in an international monetary system which, since the end of the last war, used nearly exclusively a convertible U.S. dollar not only for settlements with the United States, but also as the major intervention currency for settlements between third countries and as the major component of reserve building by all countries experiencing surpluses in their balance of payments. The temporary inconvertibility of the dollar clearly affects deeply its acceptability in all these respects, but what is there to take its place ?

The second factor is the equally temporary—but possibly due to become permanent—enlargement of the intervention margins for exchange rates from 1 per cent—actually 0.75 per cent under the European Monetary Agreement—to 2.25 per cent on either side of the newly agreed upon realigned exchange rates. A total swing of 4.5 per cent in European currencies vis-à-vis the traditional intervention currency—*i.e.* the U.S. dollar—would mean a possible swing of 9 per cent between the European currencies themselves. The European Community has reiterated, time and time again, its determination to preserve much smaller margins of fluctuations between its member currencies, and, indeed, to eliminate gradually such margins in preparation for full Monetary Union within the Community. New methods of stabilization interventions by central banks in the exchange market will clearly be needed to fulfil this objective.

Both of these factors should lead to a much earlier implementation of the European Reserve Fund initially proposed at The Hague by Chancellor Brandt, and rechristened European Fund for Monetary Cooperation in the Werner Plan and "Organisme pour une gestion concertée des réserves" by President Pompidou.

The 18 December decisions have not only increased the need and urgency of such an organization, but they have also lifted one of the major obstacles to getting it off the ground. The first prerequisite, indeed, for any resumption of progress toward any European monetary organization was the definition of an agreed constellation of intra-European exchange rates. Community action had been blocked, ever since 5 May, by continued wrangling between the French and the German Ministers of Finance about the appropriate exchange rate between the mark and the franc, on the one hand, and their relationship to the U.S. dollar, on the other. The appropriate exchange rate of the lira toward other Community currencies was also in doubt. The 18 December decisions have overcome these obstacles and established presumptive rates among all European currencies—including these of future members and of non-members—and between them and the dollar.

Progress can now be resumed toward the second objective of the Werner Plan, *i.e.* the maintenance of a modest—and declining—range of permissible fluctuations among the member currencies of the present—and of an enlarged—European Community. Moreover, the enlargement of permissible fluctuations in the dollar rate now makes it clearer than ever that the fulfilment of this objective entails the direct use of European currencies themselves—rather than the use of the dollar as an intermediary—for stabilization interventions by central banks in the exchange market. To take a simple case, if the German mark tended to exceed its agreed ceiling in relation to the French franc, on the exchange market, the preservation of the agreed margin would require—tomorrow as yesterday—sales of German marks and redemptions of French francs on the market by either or both of the two central banks concerned. But this should no longer be done indirectly through daily sales of dollars by the Bank of France and purchase of dollars by the Bundesbank. The Bundesbank would sell marks against French francs and accumulate a claim on the Bank of France rather than against the U.S. Federal Reserve System. This claim would of course :

(1) carry an exchange-rate guarantee, either in terms of the creditor's currency—the mark, in this case—or, preferably, in terms of a Community unit of account, or of SDRs ;

(2) earn appropriate interest, at a rate related to market rates, but taking into account the existence of such an exchange guarantee ;

(3) be repayable in the form of assets mutually acceptable to both the creditor and the debtor.

These repayments could always be effected in the creditor's currency—procured from the IMF, if need be, through the use of SDRs or through normal drawings on the Fund—in any other currency—including, but not exclusively, in U.S. dollars—or in gold, at any price mutually acceptable or at which such currencies or gold can be transferred into convertible claims on the IMF.

As noted already in the Werner and Ansiaux reports, these operations could be greatly streamlined and facilitated by the establishment of a European Fund. "Each country would have an account with the Fund (in lieu of bilateral accounts between each pair of central banks), and its assets or liabilities on this account would be denominated in units of account. The account would be settled from time to time by the transfer of reserves from the debtor countries to the surplus countries." The size and frequency of these eventual settlements would be greatly reduced by multilateral compensations of bilateral claims and debts, such as were made familiar to all by the highly successful operation of the European Payments Union from 1950 through 1958.

The third problem to be faced by the Community relates to the settlement of its transactions with non-member countries, and particularly to the rates of exchange between each member currency and the U.S. dollar. It is now agreed that the dollar may fluctuate up and down in terms of European currencies within a total range of 4.5 per cent. To prevent such fluctuations from introducing a similar—and unacceptable—degree of instability between the member currencies themselves, these will have to fluctuate *jointly* in terms of the dollar. The simplest way to reach this objective would be for all member central banks to avoid any intervention whatsoever on the dollar market until the dollar rises to the ceiling or falls to the floor of this 4.5 per cent range. Market arbitrage among the member currencies themselves, together with the central bank interventions already discussed above, would then ensure a parallel flotation of the dollar vis-à-vis all member currencies.

Problems of joint decisions about the dollar rate would arise, however, in two cases :

(1) If member countries decided that they prefer to buy or purchase dollars, rather than let its rate go down or up by the full amount of the permissible margin ;

(2) Unavoidably, if the dollar rate threatened to rise, or to fall, beyond the 4.5 per cent margin of permissible fluctuations. The 18 December communiqué makes it clear that the United States is not ready yet to shoulder full responsibility for keeping market fluctuations within the agreed 4.5 per cent margin by selling, or buying, itself other reserve assets against dollars. In such a case, "appropriate monetary means and *division of responsibilities* for defending stable exchange rates and for insuring *a proper degree of convertibility* of the system" (italics mine) are still listed among the unresolved issues to be tackled in Phase II of the negotiations.

A persistent weakness of the dollar on the exchange market would thus face once more the European countries with the same problem that has long confronted them and that culminated in the 5 May and 15 August crises : what amounts of inconvertible dollars would their Central Banks be ready to purchase in order to avoid—or limit—an unwanted appreciation of their currency vis-à-vis the dollar ? European firms and trade unions would once more exercise enormous pressure on their monetary and political authorities to prevent currency appreciations reducing their competitiveness at home and in world markets, especially if the weakness of the dollar arose from vast capital movements unrelated to the evolution of comparative prices and costs, and prompted instead by pure exchange-rate speculation, or even by differential movements of interest rates at home and abroad. *Joint* decisions would have been as hard to harmonize as they were since 5 May and 15 August. The reaching of such decisions and their concrete implementation would at least be facilitated by the creation of the proposed European Fund.

Fortunately, the evolution of the U.S. balance of payments is likely to provide a substantial breathing space before such a problem has to be met in practice. Interest rate developments and exchange-rate speculation have moved billions of dollars into the coffers of reluctant central banks in 1970 and 1971. The 18 December realignment of exchange rates can be expected to trigger flows of such funds back to the United States. The dollar will probably be very strong on the markets over the forthcoming months and Central Banks should not be faced, in the short run, with the need to accumulate further amounts of dollars. They should instead be able to get rid of some of the huge amounts of unwanted dollars reluctantly piled up by them over the last two years.

In the longer run, however, the balance of payments of the United States—like that of every other country—should be expected to experience again temporary deficits alternating with temporary surpluses, and the problem of more lasting and fundamental disequilibria may well emerge again. The Phase II negotiations on long-term reforms of the international monetary system should be predicated on the realistic assumption that neither the United States nor other countries will be permanently wise and lucky in the running of their own affairs, and that temporary, and even enduring, disequilibria are the rule, rather than the exception, in the worldwide pattern of international settlements.

Phase II should therefore be tackled with a feeling of real urgency, if we do not wish to expose the world again to the recurrence of the crises that plagued, and finally broke, the ill-fated gold-exchange standard of yesteryear. If acceptable and viable solutions were deferred too long, the countries of the Community—and others—would be sorely pressed to seek in various forms of exchange control an escape from the dilemma of unwanted dollar accumulation on the one hand, or unwanted—and possibly unwarranted—exchange-rate appreciation vis-à-vis the dollar on the other. If this were to happen, and particularly if the problem arose again from large movements of funds among major money and financial markets, the monetary authorities should be ready to meet them through controls jointly agreed and jointly implemented both by the countries suffering from undesirable capital outflows and those suffering from undesirable capital inflows. Temporary recourse to double-tier exchange systems—à la Swiss or à la Belgium—separating the exchange rate on trade transactions from the exchange rate on financial transactions might be a lesser evil in this respect than rigid systems of quantitative controls. Yet, the two rates could not be allowed to diverge too much without inviting widespread evasions, extremely difficult to control.

If agreement can be reached on the temporary nature of such disturbing capital movements, they could best be met by compensatory official financing, preferably through the IMF — as aimed for in the General Arrangements to Borrow—or through a broad network of multilateralized swap agreements. Enduring, but indesirable, capital movements could not be handled in this manner, but would be unlikely to persist in the absence of other disequilibrating factors calling for reconsideration of national policies and/or exchange rates.

In brief, the European Community should turn urgently toward concrete implementation of the Werner Plan, with an accelerated time-table for the measures then contemplated, and particularly for the establishment of a European Fund capable of dealing effectively with the problem of exchange rates and settlements both among its members and with nonmember countries. Joint agreements within the Community itself are a prerequisite not only for its own survival, but also for successful negotiations and agreements with other countries, including the United States. They should help both to solve the immediate problems ahead and to accelerate agreement on the worldwide issues of monetary reform enumerated in the 18 December communiqué of the Group of Ten.

III. LONGER-TERM ISSUES

First and foremost among the longer-term issues facing the Community is that of reaching agreement on the worldwide reform of the international monetary system. I shall not repeat here the suggestions developed at length in my former writings, and most recently in my article, already referred to above, in the November 1971 *Bulletin of the National Bank of Belgium.*

1. *Reserve Composition*

The keystone of such a reform should, as largely agreed already, be the use of a new type of reserve asset on the IMF—building on the SDR system—as the major form of international reserves, and the gradual phasing out of gold and reserve currencies from the system. The huge gold and foreign currency reserves inherited from the past should be converted into this new reserve asset, and holdings of foreign currencies as monetary reserves should be confined in the future to the modest "working balances" needed for stabilization interventions in the exchange market. Any foreign currencies bought from the market in the course of such interventions, but exceeding agreed ceilings (15 per cent of global reserves ?), should be promptly deposited with the IMF, credited to the depositing country's reserve account and debited from the reserve account of the country whose currency has been deposited with the Fund. Conversely, any country should be able to withdraw from its reserve account any currencies needed to replenish working balances depleted by stabilization interventions in the exchange market.

2. *The "Overhang"*

The vast amounts of foreign currency reserves—primarily dollars—inherited from more than half a century of functioning of the gold-exchange standard could not, however, and should not, be debited overnight from the debtor countries' reserve account. As indicated above, a substantial portion of the $45 to $50 billion of U.S. dollars now held by foreign central banks is likely to be absorbed by the probable repatriation of the speculative outbursts of the last two years, and another $10 billion or thereabouts to be retained as working balances. The remainder should be exchanged by the Fund for the new IMF reserve asset, but held by it as long-term investment—or even, preferably, consols—rather than debited overnight from the U.S. reserve account.

3. *Financing and/or Adjustment of Disequilibria*

Temporary disequilibria should be financed for all countries—including now the former reserve-currency countries—through fluctuations in reserve assets and/or drawings on the IMF. The United States and the United Kingdom should no longer enjoy the "exorbitant privilege" of financing their deficits through unlimited, but precarious, accumulation of their national currency as international reserves by foreign central banks. This would avoid the main source of the international monetary crises that plagued, and finally killed, the ill-fated gold exchange standard.

Persistent disequilibria call, not for financing, but for appropriate readjustments of either domestic policies or foreign exchange rates. The need for such readjustments should be recognized as a matter of common concern and be imposed upon persistent surplus countries as well as upon persistent deficit countries. I have suggested that any persistent surpluses or deficits bringing a country's reserves, let us say 25 per cent beyond, or below, "normal" should trigger automatically consultations between the country and the IMF regarding appropriate changes in domestic policies and/or exchange rates, and that if agreement cannot be reached, the Fund may be empowered to prohibit, or limit, any further interventions on the exchange market having the effect of bringing reserves, let us say 33 per cent above, or below, their normal level.

Such a suggestion might help solve the problems that may still confront the countries of an enlarged European Community during the 10 year transition period now envisaged for the completion of their Economic and Monetary Union. Exchange rates among the currencies of the European Community countries would normally be fixed within very narrow, and declining eventually to zero, margins of fluctuations. But such rates cannot be realistically considered as irrevocable until much greater progress has been achieved toward harmonization of national policies, and substantial transfers of jurisdiction and authority from national to Community institutions. Persistent failures of harmonization policies should trigger a reconsideration of the existing pattern of infra-Community exchange rates. Consultations on such readjustments could be called for by any country whose reserve increases or reserves losses (including claims or debts arising from mutual support or assistance operations) exceed an agreed percentage of the country's normal reserves, and these

Community consultations should precede the consultations with the IMF envisaged above. Since most of the Community countries' foreign trade is with one another, they would be the parties primarily affected by such exchange-rate readjustments, and any proposals for parity changes should be agreed among them before being submitted to the IMF.

Changes in official reserves should not, of course, be regarded as the only criterion determining the appropriateness of a readjustment of exchange rates. Other factors would have to be taken into account, such as the evolution of external debts and claims of the country's commercial banks, of other items—particularly merchandise exports and imports—in the country's balance of payments, comparative movements in prices and wage rates, etc. These factors should confirm, or weaken, the presumption that large and persistent reserve gains or losses should justify and require a readjustment in the country's basic exchange rate or par value.

4. *From the European Reserve Fund to a European Reserve System*

The European Reserve Fund suggested in the first section of this paper should centralize, from the very beginning, the credit lines already agreed for short-term monetary support and any further credits granted for medium-term financial assistance. Interventions in member currencies needed to keep intra-Community exchange rates within the permissible margin of fluctuations should be credited and debited in each country's account with the Fund.

Each member country should, in addition, deposit with the Fund an agreed proportion of its global gold and, particularly, foreign currency reserves. Future market interventions in dollars and/or other foreign currencies should conform to the directives of the Fund and should be credited or debited also in the country's account with the Fund. This account would therefore reflect the total evolution of each country's reserves and provide daily the information relevant to the consultations suggested under (3) above.

In the course of time, the proportion of each country's monetary reserves to be held with the Fund should be gradually increased until all reserves are held with the Fund and jointly managed by it, in preparation for the ultimate merging of their national currencies into a single European currency.

Until, and even after, that ultimate step is taken, the European Reserve System—just as the U.S. Federal Reserve System—could retain a considerable degree of autonomy for the participating national central banks. Each of these could continue to manage its own monetary and credit operations within agreed statutory limits, under the general supervision of a joint Board, or European Monetary Authority, grouping the

Governors of national Central Banks, or their deputies, and—for certain important decisions—the Ministers of Finance of the participating countries.

The statutory rules to be adopted would probably include the setting up of national credit ceilings, to be exceeded only with the approval of the European Monetary Authority, of minimum reserve ratios, and other regulatory techniques inspired from present central banking legislations in the Community and abroad, and from the experience acquired by the European Reserve Fund in the first stages of the developing Monetary Union.

An equitable distribution of the burden associated with the maintenance of adequate external reserves by the Community as a whole would probably require that each member Central Bank observe some minimum prescriptions with regard to such reserve holdings. These prescriptions might have to be met at times by the negotiation of interest-bearing, stabilization loans, at long or medium term, by the low reserve countries, either abroad or with the high reserve countries. Such loans could also be used to amortize, or rather to consolidate, the debts incurred under the provisions for mutual monetary support and financial assistance among member countries. Denominated in the Community's unit of account, they could be placed initially with the central banks of the countries with the highest levels of external reserves, but under arrangements—especially as to interest rates—facilitating their negotiation with the public, and enabling such central banks to mop up excess liquidities in their market. They could be jointly guaranteed by all member central banks and serve as a primer for the development of open-market operations throughout the territory of the Community.

The Community's unit of account would also be likely to be used more and more, in lieu of the Eurodollar, in private lending and borrowing operations. Traveler's checks denominated in the unit of account should also become more acceptable than traveler's checks denominated in dollars, since they would be subject to much smaller margins of exchange-rate fluctuations.

Finally, the European Reserve Fund itself could issue a new money market asset, denominated in the unit of account, carrying a rate of interest making it an attractive instrument for short-term investment, and usable as an intervention currency in the exchange market, in lieu of dollars or other national currencies. This suggestion is by no means an academic dream, having been made in fact by Rinaldo Ossola, the imaginative chairman of the respectable Group of Ten deputies.

The Community's unit of account could thus gradually take the place now played by the Eurodollar in the monetary and financial markets, preparing the public for its ultimate substitution for the national currencies themselves in the final stage of the European Monetary Union.

5. *Relations with the IMF*

At some stage in the development of the system—and, indeed, as early as possible—the operations of member countries with the IMF should be merged, and a single membership substituted for the separate membership of each participating country.

Until this can be accomplished, member countries should, in accordance with previous decisions of the Council of Ministers, harmonize their own policies in the IMF and consult in advance on all their borrowing and lending transactions with it and with non-member countries. Such lending and borrowing transactions should, ideally, be undertaken only to help in the settlement of global surpluses, or deficits, of the Community as a whole with the rest of the world. As long as national transactions with the Fund cannot be merged into single Community transactions, the European Monetary Authority should apportion among its members, in the light of their individual reserve positions, all proposals for Fund lending or borrowing, and all Community countries' representatives in the Fund should support such proposals in the debates of the Fund's Executive Directors.

IV. SUMMARY AND CONCLUSIONS

The agreements reached on 18 December have removed the main obstacle to the resumption of progress along the Werner Plan for European monetary unification, *i.e.* the difficulty to reach agreement on a constellation of stable—although *not* irrevocably stable, yet—exchange rates among the countries of the Community.

They have, moreover, vastly increased the need and urgency for such progress. The continued inconvertibility of the dollar and the enlargement of permissible margins of fluctuations in the dollar rate combine to make the dollar less and less usable as an intervention currency for the maintenance of the lower and declining margins of fluctuations which the Community countries wish to preserve between their own national currencies, preparatory to their merging of these separate currencies into a single Community currency.

Movement toward the Monetary Union affirmed at the summit meeting of the Hague would be greatly eased and accelerated by the early establishment of a European Reserve Fund, already agreed to in principle —under varying vocables—by all member countries.

Internally, such a Reserve Fund would provide the most appropriate instrument for the use of member currencies—rather than of a non-member currency—in the stabilization interventions needed to prevent fluctuations of intra-Community exchange rates beyond the agreed margins.

It should also be the most appropriate instrument for the gradual development of a European Reserve System, capable of reaching and implementing the multiple policy decisions needed for the completion of full monetary union among the member countries.

Externally, the European Reserve Fund should concentrate gradually into a single depository institution the holdings and management of member countries' external reserves, and facilitate joint decisions—and their implementation about interventions in the foreign exchange market for non-member currencies, particularly the dollar. It should also prepare and facilitate agreement with the United States and other foreign monetary authorities and the IMF concerning the amounts of such interventions the rates at which they should take place, and the joint elaboration and implementation of measures designed to control and/or to offset volatile movements of capital between the major money markets.

The operations of the Community countries with the IMF should be reserved to financing of global disequilibria between the Community as a whole and the outside world, while disequilibria among member countries themselves should be handled by the European Reserve Fund, thus relieving the IMF from responsibilities that can best be discharged on a regional rather than on a worldwide basis.

Ultimately, the relations of the Community countries with the IMF should be merged into a single membership, reflecting the realities of the Monetary Union of its participating countries.

The Exchange Rate Question for a United Europe: Internal Flexibility and External Rigidity versus External Flexibility and Internal Rigidity 6

Harry G. JOHNSON
The London School of Economics and the University of Chicago

INTRODUCTION: THE PROBLEM

The authors who have undertaken to prepare background papers for this Conference have been confronted by the serious difficulty that the Conference was planned before the "dollar crisis", provoked by the actions of the United States Administration on 15 August 1971, erupted, at which time there existed a fairly clearly defined and well-known system of international monetary organization. The Conference was postponed, at least partly because of the uncertainties created by that crisis ; and it is now meeting within a month of the resolution of that crisis, at least temporarily. The resolution has involved a token rise in the price of gold, a return to the previous system of fixed-exchange rates, but one which involved a substantial realignment of the relative values of the major currencies in terms of one another, and a widening at least temporarily of the band of variation of market rates of exchange around par values. But the major issues of exchange-rate flexibility which had been recognized to constitute a serious drawback of the pre-existing system have all been deferred for future consideration and negotiation, while it is not even clear that the rise in the price of gold agreed upon in the arrangements of 17 December 1971 will be accepted by the Congress of the United States. In these circumstances, it is unusually difficult to know what system of international monetary organization we are discussing, and therefore what changes in it we may be considering, let alone how to evaluate such changes and discuss their merits. Any discussion must be more than usually tentative, and dependent on explicit and probably more important implicit assumptions about the meaning and potential consequences of last year's crisis.

The title of this paper is intended to describe the major issue involved in the future monetary arrangements of the European Economic Communities once the Community has been expanded from six to ten members. The issue is whether the European countries should retain their

seriously to require a devaluation as well as a deflation or the restoration of internal and external balance. Indeed, this proposition, if it were correct, would make it a simple matter for the union to adopt a common currency or its equivalent in terms of rigidly fixed-exchange rates.

In formal theoretical terms, an answer can be provided along several possible lines. One obvious one, in terms of the theoretical models, is that in spite of industrial diversification members' manufactures are imperfectly or monopolistically competitive with one another, so that excess demand can raise the prices of exportables and importables above the level consistent with balance-of-payments equilibrium, and devaluation is an easier method than deflation and the accompanying unemployment for restoring the competitive price-relationships required for external and internal balance. An alternative explanation, consistent with the assumption of perfect competition in the pricing of traded goods, entails the assumption of a significant sector of non-traded goods and services whose prices may move independently (and may be peculiarly responsive to government demand-management policies) with inflationary developments of wages and prices in this sector communicating themselves to factor prices and the profitability of exporting and import-competing production, so that excess demand makes wages—but not prices—uncompetitive and requires again a choice between deflation of production and employment, and devaluation, as means of restoring the international competitiveness required for external and internal balance. A third explanation would appeal to ignorance, lags, and overshooting in the adjustment of domestic wages and prices to changes in demand pressure at the micro-economic level ; this explanation gains plausibility from recent research into the micro-economic foundations of the Phillips curve in the economics of wage-determination under local bargaining, which relies on the costs of information and market search. A fourth and not very intellectually satisfying explanation appeals to "noise" or stochastic elements in the operation of competition.

Meade's analysis of the problem of balance-of-payments adjustment in a free trade area (and mine also) was based on the theory of exchange-rate flexibility as it stood at that time ; and that theory implicitly identified national economies with currency areas. Contemporary analysis of the problem is based on the theory of optimum currency areas as developed by Mundell, McKinnon, and others.[5]

Mundell was primarily concerned with the question of whether the optimum currency area might not be smaller than the whole national economy, and made the optimum currency area a question of the mobility

---

[5] Robert A. Mundell, "A Theory of Optimum Currency Areas", *American Economic Review,* Vol. 51, September 1961 ; pp. 657-665, reprinted in his *International Economics,* New York, Macmillan, 1968 ; Chapter 12, pp. 177-186.

of factors of production within the area, though he recognized limits on the possibility of reducing the range of a currency area set by the necessity for money to retain its characteristic of being a form of generalized purchasing power. (Incidentally, I now think that the emphasis placed by Mundell and many other writers on regional differences in unemployment rates as an indication of non-optimality of currency arrangements is mistaken ; according to the theory of the micro-economics of labour markets mentioned above, the persistence over long historical periods of regional differences in unemployment rates represents differing equilibrium adjustments to the choice between labour and leisure.) McKinnon [6] made the question one of the "openness" of the economy, which would determine the "moneyness" of the money of the area, *i.e.* the extent to which a change in the exchange rate would not be offset by a compensating automatic increase in the domestic currency prices of tradeable goods and services. Kenen [7] subsequently attempted to make the optimum currency area a matter of the diversity and flexibility of economic activity in the area ; while Haberler, in discussions of the problem, and with the exchange-rate relationships among the major nations rather than Mundell's original problem in mind, made it a matter of the degree of similarity of the national policy objectives of governments with respect to the trade-off between inflation and unemployment.

All of these analyses contain important clues about or insights into the conditions under which either a national currency can be managed (via monetary or exchange-rate policy) to preserve external equilibrium without excessive internal regional or sectoral strains, or a group of countries can maintain fixed exchange rates or a common currency among themselves. Unfortunately, they tend to cancel each other out, so that by the end of the Chicago Conference on International Monetary Problems of 1966 [8] the theoretical problem seems to have reached a dead end of analysis. The problem has since been revived in the context of world inflation and the proposal for a common European currency, [9] but more as a concept for debate than as a fruitful theoretical foundation for policy progress. [10]

---

[6] Ronald I. McKinnon, "Optimum Currency Areas", *American Economic Review,* Vol. 53, September 1963 ; pp. 717-724.

[7] Peter B. Kenen, "The Theory of Optimum Currency Areas : An Eclectic View", in Robert A. Mundell and Alexander K. Swoboda (eds.), *Monetary Problems of the International Economy,* Chicago, University of Chicago Press, 1969 ; pp. 41-60.

[8] See the volume cited in the preceeding note.

[9] Harry G. Johnson and Alexander K. Swoboda (eds.), *The Economics of Common Currencies,* London, Allen & Unwin, 1973.

[10] It is interesting to record that Mundell has become an ardent exponent of fixed exchange rates recently.

Experience of exchange-rate problems in my judgment strongly supports Haberler's emphasis on harmony or discord of national demand-management policies as the most directly useful idea to emerge from the discussion of optimum currency areas and their crucial economic characteristics. At any rate, I shall focus on policy harmonies and discords. And I offer as a preliminary point the observation that the exchange-rate problems of recent years have been due to the interaction between a shift of United States policies from policies that produced a reasonable degree of price stability in that country to policies that produced an uncomfortable rate of price inflation, and differences among the European countries (including the United Kingdom) in their domestic tolerance for inflation and hence their willingness to accept the infusion of a U.S.-led world inflation that for some meant an undesired importation of both inflation and U.S. dollars and for others a welcome relief from the adverse balance-of-payments effects of domestic inflation necessitated by political pressures. In other words, so long as the United States maintained reasonable price stability, it suited the other major countries to live with the international financial dominance of the dollar and to retain some autonomy of domestic policy on the basis of being able to change their national exchange rates against the dollar if necessary ; once the United States became a potent source of world inflation, the question naturally arose of establishing a basis for common action to resist the importation of inflation. I shall later suggest that the key question for the future is whether the prospect of continuing inflation in the United States is sufficiently strong and sufficiently distasteful to the European countries to make them willing to adopt a common currency or its internally-rigid exchange-rate equivalent and introduce the necessary harmonization of domestic economic policies, in order to be able to counter American inflation by harmonized upward exchange-rate flexibility, or whether they will be willing to live with the dominance of the United States in the recently-restored fixed-rate system (sustained of course by the hope of gradually reducing that dominance through the extension of the Special Drawing Rights system and the funding of outstanding dollar balances) as the price of retaining more freedom of domestic policy action than would be allowed by a rigid commitment to fixed-exchange rates among the European currencies.

THE PROPOSAL FOR A COMMON EUROPEAN CURRENCY

In my admittedly jaundiced view, the proposal to establish a common European currency represents only the most recent phase of the continued efforts of the Brussels bureaucracy of the European Economic Communities—the powerful institutionalized relic of the entirely understandable and in some respects admirable post-World War II movement for European political and economic integration—to force ever further integration on countries which are no longer convinced of its political necessity [11]. After the establishment of the Common Agricultural Policy, it was widely asserted and even more widely believed that that policy ruled out any possibility of change in the exchange rates of the Common Market countries' currencies against one another, an assertion that implied that the member governments would willy-nilly have to harmonize their economic policies to the extent required to maintain internal exchange-rate rigidity. (In the light of hindsight, it can be said also to have involved the implicit assumption that American prices would remain stable, so that internal rigidity would also mean rigidity against the dollar.)

The assertion was unfounded in theory, as has frequently been shown, because differential rates of inflation among member countries distort competitive conditions among groups of national agricultural producers and the exchange-rate changes necessary to correct for them merely restore the *status quo ante*. But discrete exchange-rate changes as under the International Monetary Fund system are nonetheless disruptive, and theory suggests that flexible exchange rates would provide more continuous conditions of fair competition among farmers in the different member countries confronted with different national trends in their input costs. In fact, different price trends among the member countries, in the face of the American inflation, forced exchange-rate adjustments in the German mark and the French franc, and the temporary suspension of the Common Agricultural Policy. When it came to the test, it was the dam and not the river that gave way. The Common Agricultural Policy did not force harmonization of domestic policies, and the lack of such harmonization finally forced adjustment of exchange rates among the major European countries, while the consequences for the Common Agricultural Policy had to be met by *ad hoc* adjustments.

The Commission reacted to this setback by tackling the question of permanent fixation of intra-Community exchange rates directly, and won agreement from member governments on acceptance of the objective of

[11] An exception should be made for the United Kingdom, where membership of the European Community became an internal political necessity, in my judgment, after the disastrous failure of the Suez invasion of 1956 and the associated demonstration that neither the special relationship with the United States nor the sentimental support of the erstwhile empire any longer provided a basis for the continuance of imperial assumptions and habits of behaviour in world politics. British subscription to the objective of establishing a common European currency is to be regarded largely as a matter of acceptance of one of the many prices of membership, though of course, as a major participant in the Eurodollar market, which a common currency might hope to replace, the British financial community has, or at least thinks it has, a commercial interest in the proposal.

establishing a common currency and recognition of the implications of achieving this objective in the way of harmonization of monetary, fiscal, and other policies. This agreement, incidentally, from the point of view of the international monetary system as a whole had the extremely unfortunate effect of blocking further progress towards a systematized increase in exchange-rate flexibility generally. Such increased flexibility had come to be regarded as desirable by international monetary officialdom after the various international monetary crises that preceded the franc devaluation and mark revaluation effected very tardily in 1969. At that time, proposals for a widening of the band of permitted fluctuation of market exchange rates about the official parities, for adoption of some version of the "crawling peg" plan for automatic slow adjustment of the parities themselves to diverging price trends in national economies, and for allowing the undervalued currencies of surplus countries to be temporarily floated so that these countries could avoid the awkward problem of choosing a new parity immediately, were very much under active discussion. Determination on the objective of a common European currency, which would have to be established before it could be made flexible against the dollar, meant the shelving of discussion of these proposals, pending the establishment of the new common currency. That in turn made the dollar crisis of 1971, in some form, an inevitability: if the Europeans were confined by the common currency objective to doing nothing about the overvaluation of the dollar except complain about it, the initiative in securing a devaluation of the dollar relative to the European and Japanese currencies would necessarily fall to the Americans, and to take it they would have to rupture the established pattern of international monetary relationships.

While the notion of a common European currency originated in the desire to force real integration by winning political acceptance of the symbols of it in advance of the reality, it gained considerable additional appeal on two grounds: politically, in terms of providing a rival world currency to the dollar, an objective strengthened by the unpopularity of the war in Viet Nam; and economically, from the potentiality of countering the current American inflation and the presumed advantages to the United States of dollar-financed deficits, by revaluation or upward flotation of the common currency against the dollar. In passing, it may be noted that the economic gains to the United States from foreign holdings of dollars, and from its ability to induce expansion of those holdings by imposing inflation on the rest of the world, can very easily be vastly exaggerated by theoretical analysis based on the classical conception of money as inherently non-interest-bearing and ignoring the gains to the holder of liquid assets from financial intermediation. Most foreign-held dollars are held in forms that yield an interest return as well as a liquidity service, and the interest return tends to be adjusted upwards in face of inflation. Further, the growth of the Eurodollar market has meant that much of any "seigniorage gain" accrues to banks located in Europe rather than in America. Finally, still in passing, the arguments assume that a viable European alternative to the dollar either exists or could be quickly created—and that is precisely the problem, that its creation would require major institutional or policy changes.[12] Be that as it may, these various additional arguments have brought the concept of the optimal currency area back into the realm of discussion—and a very awkward recruit to the cause of a common European currency it has made, to be sure.

In this connection, it should be mentioned that there is a real problem that a common currency could solve if it could be implemented, namely that any individual European country that revalues to protect itself from inflation emanating from the United States has to cope with the uncertainties involved in the fact that most of its trade is conducted with other European countries rather than with the United States, so that common action would be far less disruptive of intra-European trading relationships than individual action. The problem is reminiscent of the reasons why competing oligopolies frequently find it useful to form mergers, cartels, or information-exchanging arrangements. But the problem for the European countries is to establish the foundations and mechanisms for common action against a common cause of trouble, which are now nonexistent—as proven by the inability of the European countries to respond to the American challenge to exercise world monetary leadership issued on 15 August 1971.

The absence of the preconditions necessary for the establishment of a common currency had in fact been demonstrated conclusively earlier in the year, when the Common Market countries were unable to agree on any commonly instituted alternative to the flotation of the German mark in May 1971. That policy event was in a sense more deeply symptomatic of European disunity than either the inability to agree on a common policy stance in response to the American challenge just mentioned, or the fact that the outcome of the crisis of 1971 has been a realignment of exchange rates among the European currencies as well as between them and the dollar, in place of the general and uniform appreciation against the dollar that the imposition of the uniform 10 per cent surcharge and some policy statements at the beginning of the crisis implied that the Americans were seeking. For a commitment to fixed exchange rates, sub-

[12] Mundell and others have argued for the development of the Eurodollar into a European currency; but this proposal has obvious political drawbacks from a European point of view, though some of the plans put forward for a common currency implicitly involve essentially re-naming the Eurodollar a Europa and taking over the existing financial machinery on its behalf.

ject to the safety-valve of infrequent use of revaluation or devaluation in case of necessity, puts pressure on countries to harmonize their policies and could possibly eventually produce sufficient harmonization for a binding commitment to fixed exchange rates or establishment of a common currency to be feasible and acceptable, whereas a floating rate as a non-transient arrangement removes the need for harmonization.

It may be added that both the French insistence on a rise in the dollar price of gold, and the British insistence on not appreciating as much as the Germans and Japanese in spite of their strong balance-of-payments position (with the obvious purpose of entering the Common Market with an undervalued currency so that the balance-of-payments costs involved could be absorbed without an explicit devaluation), reflect a degree of concern for purely national policy interests ominous for the prospects of establishing a common European currency with the policy harmonization and acceptance of the primacy of collective over individual national interests that that entails.

FUTURE PROSPECTS

The fixed exchange rate, Bretton Woods and International Monetary Fund, system of international monetary organization has been restored, with a new set of parities intended to represent an international consensus on equilibrium currency values sustainable for the future, though also with some concession to the earlier recognized need for more automatic flexibility of exchange rates through a widening of the band for fluctuation of market exchange rates around their parities. The fact that the wider band but not the crawling peg or temporary flotation proposal has been adopted means, however, that only a very limited concession has been made to what has been, in my judgment at least, the central problem of the system, *i.e.* the existence of divergences of national demand management policies leading to divergences of national cost and price trends requiring continuing adjustments of exchange rates.[13] The wider band is suitable for accommodating transient policy errors that will be corrected fairly speedily, transferring part of the responsibility for exchange-rate stabilizing operations to private in place of official specula-

[13] An alternative view of the problem that should perhaps be mentioned is that demand-management policies have proved incapable of preventing sporadic outbursts of wage-push inflation, and that "incomes policy" is no more promising a means to that end, so that exchange-rate flexibility is necessary to prevent "union pushfulness" from causing intractable international disequilibria. My own view is that "union pushfulness" is not an independent phenomenon but only a facet of the inflationary mechanism.

tors, and enabling central banks to impose heavier financial penalties on "unjustified" destabilizing speculation ; but it affords only small and short-run scope for exchange-rate adjustments in response to divergent national price trends.

If such divergent national price trends—resulting from divergent national choices on the trade-off function between inflation and unemployment—re-emerge there will be further international monetary crises. And there is every reason to believe that they will re-emerge. The question of relevance, however, is whether there will be greater divergences between the average of the European countries (or perhaps more accurately the average of the European countries' aspirations and tolerances) and the United States, or among the European countries themselves. If, on the one hand, as in the past five years or so, the United States chooses for itself and under the present fixed-rate system forces on the rest of the world an unreasonably high and disturbing rate of inflation, the argument for establishing a common European currency will remain strong, perhaps sufficiently so to induce the European countries to sacrifice a considerable amount of domestic policy autonomy for the sake of the policy harmonization that would be required to implement it. If, on the other hand, the United States adopts policies that will result in a return to reasonable stability of American prices, the European countries may well prefer to retain the domestic policy autonomy they have enjoyed over the postwar period on the basis of their ability to change their exchange rates against both the United States and their fellow-European countries together, while of course continuing to pay lip-service to the common currency ideal but contriving in practice to make only glacial progress towards it.

Monetary Integration in the European Common Market

7

Bela BALASSA *
Johns Hopkins University

As background to the subsequent discussion, Section I of the paper provides a short history of the attempts made to coordinate monetary policies in the EEC. In Section II the advantages and the preconditions of monetary integration are described. Consideration is further given to the implications for maintaining fixed exchange rates of national differences in "transformation functions" and "preference functions" that relate inflation, employment, and economic growth. In Section III, the advantages and disadvantages of the systems of adjustable pegs and of greater rate flexibility are evaluated with reference to "nominal" and "real" exchange rates, and the decision making process on exchange rates is analyzed. Finally, Section IV considers the policy implications of alternative exchange-rate systems and provides recommendations for the enlarged Common Market.

I. AN INTERPRETATIVE HISTORY

A Period of Stability

The Rome Treaty focuses on questions relating to the liberalization of trade and factor movements and calls for a common commercial policy of the newly established European Economic Community. No provisions are made, however, for a common economic or monetary policy in the EEC. Apart from general pronouncements on the need for coordinating

* The author is indebted to officials of the Commission of the European Economic Community for helpful discussions and for comments on an earlier version of the paper. Useful comments were also received from friends in Frankfurt, Geneva, London, and Paris. The paper was written as part of a research project financed by the National Science Foundation.

economic policies,[1] the Treaty is limited to stating that countercyclical policy and changes in the exchange rate be treated as "a matter of common concern" (Articles 103 and 107). A Monetary Committee is established "to follow the monetary situation" in the member countries and "to formulate its views" thereon, and consultations on national economic policies are envisaged.

In March 1960, the Council of Ministers of the EEC (for short, the Council) established a Countercyclical Policy Committee to provide a framework for consultations on countercyclical policies. At the same time, the Council called on the member countries to inform the EEC Commission on the general outline of those of their plans that may affect the economic situation in the partner countries, with exception made for cases when secrecy was necessary.

Considerations of secrecy may explain the fact that in March 1961 decisions on the 5 per cent revaluation of the German mark and of the Dutch guilder were taken by the individual governments without consultations. These actions, and the differences in cost-price developments which they reflected, seem to have contributed to the inclusion of provisions relating to the coordination of countercyclical and, particularly, monetary policies in the Commission's Action Programme for the second stage (1962-1966).[2]

Apart from recommending the progressive establishment of a common countercyclical policy, the Action Programme contained proposals for advance consultations by Central Bank Governors and Finance Ministers on all actions concerning money creation, as well as on international monetary policy, including the use of IMF facilities, and on parity changes. Nevertheless, the thrust of the Action Programme was the coordination of structural[3] rather than countercyclical policies. In fact, the question of monetary policy coordination was raised in relation to the

[1] "It shall be the aim of the Community, by establishing a Common Market and progressively approximating the economic policies of Member States to promote throughout the Community a harmonious development of economic activities, a continuous and balanced expansion, an increased stability, an accelerated raising of the standard of living, and closer relations between its Member States" (Article 2; cf. also Articles 6 and 105).

[2] Memorandum of the Commission on the Action Programme of the Community for the Second Stage, Brussels, 24 October 1962 (hereinafter referred to as Action Programme).

[3] The Action Programme includes sectoral, agricultural and regional policies under this heading; in a wider sense they comprise competition, transportation, energy, and social policies which are also discussed in detail in the Programme.

common agricultural policy whose success, and ultimately that of the Common Market, was said to depend on the fixity of exchange rates.[4]

The Council of Ministers did not react to the Commission's recommendations on short-term policy coordination until after the Italian currency crisis. Following a deterioration of the Italian balance of payments, the lira came under considerable speculative pressure in late 1963 and early 1964. Instead of relying on her EEC partners, however, the Italian government, in March 1964, asked for, and received, help from the United States in the form of support from the U.S. Treasury in the foreign-exchange market, loans from the Export-Import Bank and the Commodity Credit Corporation, and a swap agreement with the Federal Reserve Bank of New York. U.S. financial assistance to Italy far overshadowed swaps with European central banks, let alone the central banks of the EEC countries.

To avoid repetition of the Italian events, in April 1964 the Council recommended that a member country, whose balance-of-payments deficit could not be financed from its own reserves, should seek "a Community solution" in financing this deficit. In the following month, it established a Fiscal Policy Committee, "to examine and to confront the general lines of fiscal policy" of the member countries, as well as a Committee of the Governors of Central Banks, to hold consultations on the general lines of credit policy in the member countries and to regularly exchange information on the measures taken by the individual central banks. The consultations were to precede the taking of such measures if "the circumstances and, particularly, the timing, of the measures so permit". Finally, the Council called for advance consultations on matters of international monetary policy, as well as on parity changes.

Subsequently, in October 1964, the Commission proposed various actions aimed at establishing a monetary union of the EEC, but such actions were not taken in the years following. Rather, emphasis was again given to structural policies, and the medium-term economic programme adopted by the Council of Ministers for the period 1966-1970 considered monetary and credit policy only to the extent these affect the movement of capital among the member countries.[5]

---

[4] "Any major modification [in exchange rates] would so much upset the trade of countries no longer protected by any customs barrier, and, because of the guaranteed Community intervention price for grain and other basic agricultural products, would cause such sudden changes in prices of farm products and therefore in farm incomes also, that the Common Market itself could be imperilled", see Action Programme, p. 128.

[5] "Programme de politique économique à moyen terme (1966-1970)", *Journal officiel des Communautés européennes* (for short, *J.O.*), No. 79, 25 August 1967, Chapter III, par. 14.

The question of exchange-rate parities was not raised in the programme and, in later pronouncements, the arguments first put forward in the Action Programme were repeatedly invoked to the effect that parity changes among EEC currencies had to be foregone, lest the common agricultural policy, and the existence of the Common Market, be jeopardized. Nor was it thought that the maintenance of existing parities would encounter difficulties in the Common Market.

Currency Crisis and Efforts for Policy Coordination

The widely expressed belief on the need to maintain unchanged parities among Common Market currencies, and on the possibility of doing so, can be understood if considered against the background of international monetary stability during the first decade of the EEC's existence. As described in more detail below, during this period the major deficit countries found ways other than devaluation to cope with their balance-of-payments problems : the United States financed its deficits largely by increasing its liabilities denominated in terms of U.S. dollars while Britain applied a stop-and-go policy to safeguard the exchange rate. In turn, apart from the 1964 crisis in Italy, the Common Market countries ran comfortable surpluses and accumulated reserves. Nor did speculation against sterling appreciably affect foreign-exchange markets in these countries ; speculation was concentrated in London and occurred mostly in sterling-dollar relationships.

In such circumstances there was little pressure for policy coordination in the Common Market as it was assumed that parities could and would be maintained without such coordination. The situation was well described in retrospective by Raymond Barre, the Vice-President of the EEC Commission for Economic and Financial Affairs, whose statement deserves full quotation [6] :

> "During the last ten years the considerable progress made in the establishment of a customs union and in the field of agriculture engendered the feeling that monetary manipulations have become unlikely, if not impossible. The fixing of common agricultural prices, their expression in forms of a unit of account, reinforced this feeling so much more that economic and monetary relationships within the Community were harmonious between 1960 and 1967, at least in appearance. A climate of false security was created, and this explains that insufficient attention was given to the coordination of economic policies and to monetary solidarity in the Community."

---

[6] "Exposé de M. Barre au Parlement européen sur la situation économique de la Communauté au début de 1970", Strasbourg, 9 February 1970.

The situation changed with the rising German surplus in 1967, when the recession led to an absolute decline in labor costs and export prices in Germany as against continuing increases elsewhere. In the second half of the year, there was speculation on the devaluation of the pound as well as on the revaluation of the mark. In November, the pound was devalued by 14.3 per cent but speculation on the revaluation of the mark continued and it intensified after the May 1968 events in France.

In the months following, there was much discussion of a possible devaluation of the French franc and revaluation of the German mark, as a means of re-establishing equilibrium in the balance of payments of the two countries and to end rampant speculation. Instead, in November 1968, France and Germany unilaterally introduced a variety of measures aimed at redressing their balance-of-payments positions without parity changes. Germany applied taxes on exports and rebates on imports at a rate of 4 per cent and imposed limitations on foreign deposits, whereas France introduced exchange controls, applied import quotas on commodities representing about one-fifth of its imports from EEC member countries, and gave aids to exports.

The lack of coordination of these measures and the purely formal character of consultations, in turn, provided incentives for seeking the coordination of monetary policies in the Common Market. A memorandum to this effect from the Commission to the Council, dated 5 December 1968, received favorable response and was followed a few months later by the submission of the so-called Barre Plan. They recommended advance consultations on countercyclical policies ; the establishment of short-term and medium-term credit facilities ; and the coordination of medium-term policies in the EEC. An important and novel feature of the Barre Plan was the emphasis on the need for relating medium-term and short-term economic policies.[7]

In July 1969 the Council expressed its agreement with several of the recommendations contained in the Barre Plan, including the establishment of short-term credit facilities for the Common Market. Furthermore, it issued a decision on the Commission's proposition to coordinate short-term economic policies, albeit with a change in wording, so that advance consultations are called for in the event that the policies of a member country have an "important effect" rather than "an effect" on the eco-

[7] "Commission Memorandum to the Council on the Co-ordination of Economic Policies and Monetary Co-operation Within the Community", Brussels, 12 February 1969, in Supplement to *Bulletin of the European Communities* 1969 (3) (hereinafter referred to as *BEC*).

nomies of other EEC countries or on their internal and external equilibrium.[8]

A few weeks later, on 8 August, France devalued the franc by 12.5 per cent without consulting its Common Market partners although such consultations were called for already by a Council decision of 1964 and its action affected the external equilibrium of the partner countries.[9] Subsequently, on 29 September, Germany adopted a floating exchange rate in opposition to the Commission. A new parity, representing an 8.5 per cent revaluation of the mark, was established on 25 October.

These events again provided an inducement for increasing policy coordination in the Common Market and on 1-2 December 1969 a Conference of the Heads of Governments was held in the Hague. While the Conference did not follow the suggestions of the Commission to consider the need for strengthening Community institutions and for progressing towards a political union, it dealt with the actions to be taken to "complete, reinforce, and enlarge" the Common Market. The final communiqué calls for the preparation of a plan, to be based on the Barre Plan, for creating in stages an economic and monetary union.

In the months following, a number of actions were taken to implement the decisions of the Hague Conference. The Council of Ministers approved the procedures for the consultations envisaged by its 17 July 1969 decision and established a system of short-term credit facilities (26 January) ; the Commission submitted a communication to the Council on the elaboration of a plan establishing in stages an economic and monetary union (4 March) ; and the Council charged a high-level group, consisting of the Presidents of the Monetary, Countercyclical, Fiscal, Medium-Term Economic Policy, and Central Bank Governors' Committees of the EEC and the General Director for Monetary and Financial Affairs of the Commission, and presided over by P. Werner, the Prime Minister of Luxembourg, to prepare a report on the creation of such a union (6 March). The Werner Committee submitted a preliminary report in May and its final report in October 1970.

---

[8] The expressions in the original French text are "une incidence notable" rather than "une incidence". See *Décision du Conseil du 17 juillet 1969, relative à la coordination des politiques à court terme.*

[9] It has been reported that the French decision for devaluation was taken on 16 July, the day before the Council issued its decision on advance consultations (*The Economist,* 16 August 1969, p. 48). It may be added that, following the devaluation, France was provided with short-term credit facilities, of which the United States offered as much as the Common Market countries taken together.

It was proposed that the first stage of establishing an economic and monetary union—1970-1971 in the Commission's original proposal [10] and 1971-1973 in the Werner Report [11]—be devoted to increasing the co-ordination of economic policies among the member countries. The Werner Report also declared the final objective to be the establishment of an economic and monetary union and proposed setting up a "centre de décision" for economic policy on the Common Market level as well as a Community-wide system of Central Banks similar to the Federal Reserve System in the United States.

The Commission marked its general agreement with the recommendations of the Werner Report for the first stage. However, it expressed the view that one should not prejudge the future division of powers between the institutions of the EEC and the national governments by proposing the establishment of a "center of decision-making" on the Community level. It further eliminated the proposition of the Werner Committee that called for an intergovernmental conference before the end of the first stage to make the necessary changes in the Rome Treaty. [12] The weakened statement on the institutional aspects of the proposed economic and monetary union in the Commission's text responded to the desire of France, which wished to avoid making a commitment for the setting up of supranational institutions. [13]

After protracted negotiations, during which Germany and several other countries upheld the conclusions of the Werner Report, and as a result of French insistence, the statement on the possible need for institutional changes was weakened further in the Council's resolution of 8-9 February 1971. In turn, in order to avoid continuing financial commitments in the absence of progress towards the unification of economic and monetary policies, Germany prevailed in introducing a safeguard clause in the resolution. According to this clause, the provisions on

---

[10] "Communication of the Commission to the Council on the Elaboration of a Plan for the Phases Etablishment of An Economic and Monetary Union", Brussels, 4 March 1970 (hereinafter referred to as A Plan for an Economic and Monetary Union), in Supplement to *BEC,* 1970 (3).

[11] "Report to the Council and the Commission on the realization by stages of Economic and Monetary Union in the Community", Luxembourg, 8 October 1970 (hereinafter referred to as the Werner Report), in Supplement to *BEC,* 1970 (11).

[12] "Commission Memorandum and Proposals to the Council on the Establishment by Stages of Economic and Monetary Union", Brussels, 30 October 1970, in *BEC,* 1970 (11), Chapter II.

[13] In commenting on the Werner Report, Maurice Schumann, the French Foreign Minister, declared : "We must avoid supranational over-bidding. We must begin by completing the first stage before we think of anything else. We must avoid getting tangled up in institutional red tape..." Statement made on 16 November 1970 and quoted in *BEC,* 1971 (1), p. 145.

reductions in the margin of fluctuations among Common Market currencies, on the establishment of a medium-term financing scheme, and on the creation of a European Reserve Fund, envisaged in the Council's resolution, will lapse if by 1975 there is no agreement on the measures of policy coordination to be taken in the second stage.

At the same time, the Council adopted the third medium-term economic programme for the period 1971-1975 ; established a system of triannual meetings on short-term economic policies ; and called for strengthening cooperation among the central banks of the member countries. The agreement on increased consultations during the first stage is, however, far from revolutionary. The proposed consultations do not involve coercion and differ from earlier arrangements mainly to the extent that a fixed time-table is now provided.

In these circumstances, only experience can show the practical importance of the consultations. In commenting on the Council's resolution, an editorial in *Le Monde* noted the scepticism of experts as to the efficacy of intergovernmental meetings on policy coordination and expressed the fear that "nothing of importance will be done in this field in the course of the first stage". [14] The events of the year 1971 did not belie these predictions.

The Crisis of 1971

Following strong speculative activity, on 5 May 1971, Germany, Belgium and the Netherlands suspended operations in foreign-exchange markets. In response to these actions, the Commission called for maintaining existing parities and for handling the "speculative crisis" by regulating the Eurodollar market through the joint action of the Central Banks of the member countries ; by reducing domestic liquidity ; and by increasing the margins of exchange rate fluctuations vis-à-vis the dollar from 0.75 to 1.0 per cent while reducing margins among Common Market currencies. [15] The Commission's recommendations were not accepted by Germany and the Netherlands which floated their currencies while France and Italy retained fixed rates and Belgium reinforced its double market for foreign-exchange transactions.

The Council of Ministers took note of these actions and admitted the use of wider margins of exchange-rate fluctuations for a limited period

---

[14] "Les meilleurs experts sont assez sceptiques sur l'efficacité des réunions sur la coordination des politiques budgétaires et économiques qui vont se multiplier à Bruxelles ... on peut craindre que rien de très significatif ne soit fait dans ce domaine au cours de la première étape", *Le Monde,* 11 February 1971.

[15] Statement by Mr. Barre to the European Parliament, 18 May 1971, in *BEC,* 1971 (6), pp. 19-23.

after which member countries should return to the original parities. It also called for the application of measures to control capital flows, and agreed to instituting compensating taxes and subsidies on agricultural trade to offset fluctuations in exchange rates.[16] In turn, the first reduction in margins of exchange-rate fluctuations between Common Market currencies, set for June 1971, was postponed *sine die.*

Following the measures taken on 15 August by President Nixon, suspending the convertibility of the U.S. dollar into gold and imposing an import surcharge, the German government suggested a joint floating of EEC currencies. The Benelux countries were sympathetic to the proposal, but it was rejected by the French. Instead, France adopted a two-market system whereas Belgium engaged in joint floating with the Netherlands.

Subsequently, on 13 September, the Council of Ministers called for establishing new fixed parities and for taking measures to hinder speculative capital flows. New parities were in fact established by the agreement of the major industrial countries on 18 December 1971, but no regulations were adopted on short-term capital movements. Compared to their gold value prior to 5 May 1971, the new parities entailed a revaluation of 4.6 per cent of the German mark and 2.8 per cent of the Belgian franc and the Dutch guilder, no change for the French franc, and a 1 per cent devaluation of the Italian lira. Among other major currencies, the U.S. dollar was devalued by 7.9 per cent, the Japanese yen revalued by 7.7 per cent, while the British pound remained unchanged. At the same time, the margins of exchange-rate fluctuations were increased from 0.75 per cent to 2.25 per cent vis-à-vis the U.S. dollar.

II. A PERMANENT FIXING OF PARITIES IN THE EEC?

The Policy Assumptions of Monetary Integration

The example of the United States shows the benefits that can be derived from monetary integration.[17] One of these is simply the ease of transactions. Furthermore, the absence of an exchange risk reduces uncertainty in trade and investment, eliminates the cost of forward transactions, and is conducive to long-term planning. The lack of possibility of exchange-rate changes also lessens the risk associated with capital and

[16] Council Resolution of 9 May 1971 concerning the Monetary Situation, in *BEC,* 1971 (6), pp. 26-27.

[17] The hallmark of monetary integration as defined here is a permanent, unalterable fixity of parities. It may or may not entail the use of a common currency.

labor movements. Also, with exchange-rate speculation precluded, capital flows will tend to remedy short-term imbalances.[18]

But the benefits of monetary integration are enjoyed in the United States in a highly interdependent economy and in a particular policy frame. Economic interdependence is reflected in the free flow of goods, capital, and labor in an economy where differences in tastes are relatively unimportant, and capital and labor markets are integrated. In turn, the policy frame includes central decision-making on monetary and fiscal policies, the use of automatic and discretionary stabilizers, and the acceptance of the policy implications of fixed exchange rates.

Similarity in tastes and the lack of obstacles to trade since the development of manufacturing industries have led to a considerable degree of regional specialization of American industry. This, in turn, assures that price trends will not diverge among regions as price differences for particular products cannot exceed the cost of transportation. Furthermore, with national wage bargaining in most major industries, wage developments cannot get out of line in various parts of the United States. Nor can interest rates differ given the existence of an integrated capital market, and the management of monetary policy on the federal level.

Monetary policy is managed by the Federal Reserve Board which keeps differences in discount rates between Federal Reserve districts within narrow limits. Monetary policy as well as the federal budget are used as instruments of countercyclical policy on the national economy level. At the same time, automatic and discretionary measures associated with the federal budget are utilized to assist regions in difficulties.

Depressed regions benefit from automatic fiscal stabilizers in the form of lower taxes and higher welfare payments, as well as from discretionary measures, some of which become automatic when a region is declared "a depressed area". But while efforts are made to alleviate the difficulties of such regions, it is considered acceptable that income differences persist and lead to out-migration. Migration, in fact, becomes an equilibrating factor in the regional adjustment mechanism.[19]

---

[18] As Ingram expressed it, in the United States short-term imbalances entailing the flow of Federal funds can be remedied by the sales and purchase of government and private securities. James C. Ingram, "State and Regional Payments Mechanisms", *Quarterly Journal of Economics,* Vol. 73, November 1959 ; pp. 619-632.

[19] However, in depressed regions capital movements tend to be disequilibrating as there is likely to be an outflow rather than an inflow of capital. By contrast, long-term capital movements act as an equilibrating factor in the event that balance-of-payments deficits are due to excessive aggregate demand. This is the case considered by Tibor Scitovsky in *Economic Theory of Western European Integration,*

The permanent fixing of exchange rates within the United States is thus associated with national wage and price determination, central decision-making on monetary and fiscal policy, the use of automatic and discretionary measures, and the acceptance of the policy implications of fixed exchange rates for individual regions. If these conditions were fulfilled in the European Common Market, monetary integration could take place there also. Central decision-making on monetary and fiscal policy, however, presupposes political integration which can be considered only a long-term goal for the Common Market. The question is then what arrangements may be adopted in the period preceding political unification.

Putting it differently, the question arises if it is possible and desirable to forego changes in exchange parities before political integration is accomplished. To answer this question, one has to consider the implications of intercountry differences in the evaluation of various policy objectives (the "preference function" of decision-makers) and in the physical trade-offs among these objectives (the "transformation function" understood in a broad sense), as well as the possibilities for policy coordination in the presence of such differences.

National Differences and Policy Coordination

The literature on the Phillips curve has accustomed us to thinking in terms of two policy objectives : price stability and full employment. We would then have a transformation function indicating possible trade-offs between the two, as well as a preference function expressing their relative evaluation by the decision-makers. While this may appear rather simple, the transformation function itself is the outcome of decisions made by economic agents as it reflects the attitude of labor unions towards unemployment and the reactions of employers to wage claims. In turn, the preference function will express the valuation of these objectives by the decision-makers who are influenced by the views of various segments of the population.[20]

Stanford, Stanford University Press, 1958, Part III. For an overview of the regional adjustment process, see my *The Theory of Economic Integration,* Homewood, Ill., R. D. Irwin, 1961, Ch. 12, and Marina von Neumann Whitman, *International and Interregional Payments Adjustment : A Synthetic View,* Princeton Studies in International Finance, No. 19, Princeton, N.J., 1967.

[20] Serge-Christophe Kolm has pointed out to me an application of this function in a model built for France. R. Guesnerie and P. Malgrange, *Formalisation des objectifs à moyen terme. Application au VIe Plan,* Paris, CEPREMAP, 1971 (mimeo).

There is no reason to assume that the transformation and preference functions as between inflation and employment would be identical among the Common Market countries. In fact, it is generally believed that there are differences in this regard among these countries. Thus, it has been said that its experience with two postwar inflations has made the Germans wary of inflation whereas the French attach greater importance to avoiding unemployment. The situation is less clear-cut in Italy while in the United Kingdom, a prospective member of the Community, the Conservative Government's desire to slow down inflation seems to be checkmated by the propensity of the unions to demand large wage increases notwithstanding high unemployment. The unions tend to be less intransigent when the Labour Party is in power but this party also values differently the objectives of price stability and full employment.

The last observations lead to the question of intercountry differences in the attitudes of labor unions. Trade union pressure is said to be stronger in France than in Germany, reflecting the hostility of the French Communist Party to the capitalist system and its influence on the labor unions. Finally, in Italy, local unions have repeatedly conducted strikes disapproved by their federation and by the Communist Party.

The attitude of employers towards wage claims will in turn greatly depend on their ability to raise prices. Such ability is related to the size of the domestic economy and to the probability of the government taking measures aimed at offsetting the effects of price increases on foreign trade. The smaller the country's national economy, the less can wage increases be translated into higher prices, hence we would expect employers to offer greater resistance to wage increases in Belgium and the Netherlands than in France, Germany, or the United Kingdom. Nonetheless, this restraint, and the incomes policy managed jointly by the government and the federations of industry and labor, failed to work in the Netherlands in periods of over-full employment.

In responding to wage claims, business will also consider the chances of the government resorting to devaluation or to trade and foreign-exchange restrictions instead of adopting a deflationary policy. Here again, past experience suggests the existence of differences among the EEC countries, with the French choosing devaluation twice (1958 and 1969) and trade and foreign-exchange restrictions once (1968) since the signing of the Rome Treaty, and Italy applying severe deflationary measures in 1964.

The analysis loses in simplicity and gains in realism if we consider the effects of past price increases, and of expectations for future increases, on the trade-off between inflation and unemployment. This will also mean that, apart from intercountry differences in the transformation and preference functions under *ceteris paribus* assumptions, one would have to take account of differences in the "initial conditions" in terms of inflationary trends and expectations and in the political and social setting.

Nor can we limit alternatives and policy goals to price stability and full employment, both of which relate to the present, but we should also consider changes in the availability of goods and services over time, *i.e.* economic growth. There may now be a trade-off between growth and price stability ; in fact, there is some evidence that, excluding cases of hyperinflation, rates of economic growth and price increases tend to be positively correlated.[21]

This result may be explained by reference to the structural changes that accompany rapid growth while contributing to inflation through creating imbalances in particular markets. It has also been argued that inflation tends to raise saving rates by redistributing incomes from low to high savers and provides incentives to investment in physical assets. Finally, to the extent that it is associated with higher employment, inflation may augment the growth potential of the economy, though there will be a trade-off between full employment and growth if measures aimed at reducing unemployment adversely affect the efficiency of resource allocation and reduce savings.

It cannot be assumed that these trade-offs would be the same for every country, just as preferences between growth and price stability or unemployment differ from country to country. For example, in countries at lower levels of development, such as Italy, higher rates of inflation may be associated with a particular growth rate since structural changes take place in the process of economic growth, and such countries may also aim at higher growth rates in order to catch up with other Common Market nations. At the same time, relatively high import propensities and demand elasticities in trade within the EEC augment the effects of differential price and growth trends on the balance of payments of the member countries while reducing the effectiveness of domestic policy instruments used to redress the balance.

It would appear, then, that given the intercountry differences in the transformation and the preference functions, the attainment of the optimal combination of growth, employment, and price stability in the individual Common Market countries is not compatible with balance-of-payments equilibrium under fixed exchange rates. This conclusion is strengthened if we consider that, with the entry of the United Kingdom, Denmark, Ireland, and Norway, the EEC will have ten member countries, and it will also gain in diversity.

---

[21] A. P. Thirlwall and C. A. Barton, "Inflation and Growth : The International Evidence", *Banca Nazionale del Lavoro Quarterly Review,* September 1971 ; pp. 263-275.

Maintaining immutably fixed exchange rates would accordingly entail compromising national objectives and foregoing the use of a policy instrument. In practical terms, this would mean that some countries *(e.g.* France) [22] would have to accept more unemployment; others *(e.g.* Germany) more inflation; [23] and again others a lower growth rate than considered desirable. In countries where balance-of-payments equilibrium requires maintaining economic activity at less than desired levels, this would also exacerbate regional problems. While such imbalances conflict with national interests, in the present situation they are not remedied by common action on the EEC level.

The question arises then whether despite the conflicts in national interests, balance-of-payments equilibrium under fixed exchange rates could be maintained in the Common Market through policy coordination in the form of consultations that are envisaged for the first stage of establishing an economic and monetary union. In this connection, past experience with consultations in the EEC is of interest.

If one inquires as to the single most important case when policy consultations have been successful in the sense that they have importantly affected the policies followed by the member countries, the case of the anti-inflationary measures taken in 1964 is often cited. At that time, the Council's recommendations for the application of anti-inflation policies, made at the behest of the Commission, were adopted by the member countries.

The success of consultations in 1964 can be explained if we consider that the Commission's recommendations corresponded to the views of the governments on the need to slow down inflation. In effect, governments appear to have welcomed the recommendations so as to make unpopular measures more palatable. In other words, since the national interests as seen by the governments largely coincided, consultations in the EEC framework were used to support the positions of individual governments.

Different considerations apply to cases when the interests of the member countries are in conflict. In such instances, the national interest has generally prevailed. The conclusions of the Werner Report continue to apply in this regard: "In general, the consultation procedures have not yielded the results expected, either because they have been of a purely formal character or because the member States have taken refuge in escape clauses." [24]

---

[22] On the inflationary bias of the French economy, see Alain Chenicourt, *L'inflation ou l'anticroissance,* Paris, Laffont, 1971.

[23] According to the 1964 report of the German Economic Advisory Council, "It is a political question if integration at fixed exchange rates justifies the sacrifice of foregoing price stability", Jahresgutachten 1964 des Sachverständigenrates, par. 241.

[24] Werner Report, p. 8.

This state of affairs was well expressed by Raymond Barre in explaining the lack of a community-wide solution to the crisis of May 1971 :[25]

> "This situation . . . derives from the dissimilarity of the situations and consequently of the interests, of the various countries within the Community, from disagreement among member countries on economic doctrine, and from differing viewpoints on the methods to be used to solve international monetary problems.
>
> So long as the Member States do not arrive at some measure of political consensus on certain major problems, we shall always have to live—despite declarations of principle expressing good intentions—with qualified commitments and, in difficult situations, with decisions designed mainly to safeguard what each country considers to be its own vital interests."

In fact the experience of the period since the Common Market's establishment points to the existence of a "policy-coordination cycle". The issue of policy coordination is neglected during periods of calm, it is raised following a crisis, but attempts to coordinate policies are jeopardized when a new crisis erupts.

This situation is a reflection of the political decision-making process that is national in character and it indicates that under present circumstances the welfare costs of maintaining immutably fixed exchange rates are not acceptable to the member countries. One may add that, with the decision-making powers remaining on the national level, the difficulties of policy coordination will tend to increase further following the accession of new members to the Common Market.

Automatic Convergence

The framework used in the discussion so far has been a national one in which the possibilities open to a country are determined domestically. However, the national economies of the Common Market countries are interdependent through trade that is not subject to duties. At the same time, it has been suggested that countries whose national economies are interdependent may form an optimum currency area since the possibilities for divergent price-trends will be reduced.[26]

---

[25] Statement by Mr. Barre to the European Parliament, 18 May 1971, and reprinted in *BEC,* 1971 (6), p. 22. Cf. also the reported remarks of the German Chancellor made at the time of the floating of the mark: "There are times", the German Chancellor, Herr Brandt told his countrymen on television at the weekend, "when Germany has to put its own interest first", *The Economist,* 15 May 1971, p. 88.

[26] Ronald I. McKinnon, "Optimum Currency Areas", *American Economic Review,* September 1963 ; pp. 717-724.

But how to measure interdependence? Calculating the ratio of exports or imports to GNP is not an appropriate indicator, in part because exports and imports are expressed in value terms while GNP is value added, and in part because GNP includes non-traded goods. As most traded goods are manufactured products, one may suggest using the share of exports in manufacturing output or that of imports in the consumption of manufactured goods as an indicator of interdependence. Data for 1968 show the share of imports from partner countries in the consumption of manufactured goods to be 34.2 per cent in Belgium-Luxemburg, 8.3 per cent in France, 6.2 per cent in Germany, 7.7 per cent in Italy and 33.1 per cent in the Netherlands.[27]

These figures indicate the dependence of Belgium-Luxemburg and the Netherlands on their Common Market partners as well as the relative independence of France, Germany and Italy. While comparable data for U.S. regions are not available, information on the location of industries suggests the existence of important differences in economic structure between the principal U.S. regions on the one hand, and the larger EEC countries on the other. Thus, while in the United States major industries such as textiles, shoes, automobiles and steel are concentrated regionally, each of the three large EEC countries, as well as a prospective entrant, Britain, has a full complement of industries.

Also, the elimination of duties on intra-EEC trade notwithstanding, a variety of factors, such as differences in tastes, in product specifications, and in technical requirements, the difficulties of establishing subsidiaries, and the maintenance of border formalities, continue to discourage trade and thus limit the interdependence of the national economies of the EEC countries. These factors are absent within the United States; they are also of lesser importance in U.S.-Canadian relationships and Canada derives about one-fifth of its consumption of manufacturing goods from imports originating in the United States. Nevertheless, Canada finds it desirable to maintain exchange-rate flexibility vis-à-vis the U.S. dollar.

A possible test of the effect of interdependence on prices is to compare the rates of increase of prices among the EEC countries and between member and non-member countries during the period following the Common Market's establishment. The data of Table 1 do not show a convergence of price increases among the EEC countries; nor have these countries experienced more similar price movements than the other major industrial nations.

At any rate, the greater uniformity of price movements by itself would not guarantee balance-of-payments equilibrium under fixed exchange

---

[27] Edwin M. Truman, *The Impact of the EEC on Trade and Production of Manufactured Goods: The First Decade*, 1971 (mimeo).

rates. This is because, as long as the process of wage determination differs from country to country, trends in profits will vary among countries and will influence investment and trade.

In this connection, note that differences in wage trends among Common Market countries are not attenuated by migration that is limited by a variety of factors, including differences in customs and language. In turn, direct investment and the movement of long-term capital are hindered by legal obstacles, so that the Common Market does not meet Mundell's test of the integration of factor markets.[28] Conversely, there are substantial funds available for short-term movements in search of gains from exchange-rate changes.

A further question is whether preference functions will become more similar over time. The national medium-term programmes, prepared for the period 1970-1975, indicate some convergence in national targets for price increases, unemployment, and the rate of growth of GNP within the Benelux taken as a unit. There is no indication of convergence, however, between the Benelux, France, Germany and Italy. In particular, the projected range in the average annual rate of increase of the GNP deflator varies between 2.2 per cent in Germany and 4.0 per cent in Belgium and the Netherlands (Table 2).

These differences, leading to a cumulated discrepancy of over 10 percentage points between countries with the smallest and the largest price increases over the period of projection, are hardly compatible with balance-of-payments equilibrium under fixed exchange rates.[29] And while it has been reported that price expectations in Germany are on the rise,[30] Germany has experienced an acceleration of inflation with subsequent deceleration once before,[31] and other countries may also show deviations from the projections just as it happened in the period 1965-1970 (Table 2).

The need for parity changes increases further if we consider the adjustments that will take place in connection with the enlargement of the Community. This will be the case especially in Britain where food prices are

[28] Robert A. Mundell, "A Theory of Optimum Currency Areas", *American Economic Review,* Vol. 51, September 1961 ; pp. 657-665.

[29] The recommendations of the expert group charged with the preparation of the medium-term programme and the programme adopted by the Council call for reducing differences in rates of price increases by the action of the national governments (Table 2). This would involve, however, overruling national preferences and there is no indication that countries would be prepared to do so.

[30] *The Economist,* 13 September 1971 ; p. 73.

[31] Annual increases in industrial prices between 1962 and 1968 were: 0.5 per cent, 1.1 per cent, 2.4 per cent, 1.8 per cent, -0.9 per cent, and -5.6 per cent, *International Financial Statistics,* 1971 Supplement.

expected to rise by about 16 per cent as a result of entry [32] and the financial contribution to the EEC, as well as loss of Commonwealth preferences, impose an additional burden on the balance of payments.

III. MONETARY ARRANGEMENTS FOR THE TRANSITIONAL PERIOD

Nominal and Real Exchange Rates

The preceding considerations explain that the Common Market countries have not assumed obligations to permanently fix exchange rates among them during the seventies, and that the need for changes in parities during this period is now generally admitted. The question is then what kind of monetary arrangements should be adopted until the conditions for the permanent fixing of exchange rates are fulfilled. Possible alternatives include the system of adjustable pegs, fully flexible exchange rates, and the crawling peg. [33]

The EEC Commission has steadfastly maintained its support of the adjustable peg system. According to the Commission, the operation of the Common Market necessitates fixed exchange rates and greater flexibility in the rates would present serious disadvantages. The case for adjustable pegs was succinctly expressed by Raymond Barre : [34]

> "The stability of exchange rates is in fact a necessary condition of the functioning of the Common Market and the creation of an economic and monetary union. It is not required only by the rules of the common agricultural policy. It is a factor in the security of transactions, the optimal orientation of capital movements, and the development of intra-community investments. It greatly encourages the efforts made for the convergence of economic policies. It assures the credibility of the Community venture. Certainly there may be

---

[32] *The United Kingdom and the European Communities,* Cmnd 4715, London, 1971.

[33] A variety of suggestions have been made as to the appropriate magnitudes and intervals for exchange rate changes under the "crawl". In the following, I will consider the case where the maximum annual change in the exchange rate of any particular country is two per cent and it occurs in steps smaller than one-tenth of one per cent. (For an early argument in favor of this crawling peg, see John H. Williamson, *The Crawling Peg,* Essays in International Finance, No. 50, Princeton, International Finance Section, December 1965.)

[34] *Perspectives de l'Union économique et monétaire dans la Communauté économique européenne,* discours prononcé par M. Raymond Barre à Zurich, le 5 juillet 1971, à l'Institut suisse de recherches internationales, pp. 7-8.

situations of fundamental disequilibrium when a parity change becomes necessary. One should not exclude a devaluation in the case of a substantial deficit in the balance of payments, nor a revaluation if there are considerable surpluses in the basic balance of payments. In such instances, necessity becomes the law. But changes in the parity should be the exception, the stability of exchange rates the rule; the defense of this stability should not be sacrificed to short-term considerations which are accidental rather than fundamental."

In the discussions, use has furthermore been made of the traditional arguments against greater exchange-rate flexibility, such as uncertainty in trade and investment, risk of speculation, and the tendency to more rapid inflation due to the removal of the balance-of-payments constraint. Other arguments specific to the EEC have been the need for fixed exchange rates for the optimal movement of capital and labor, the constraining effect of fixed rates for policy harmonization, and the desire to reduce the role of the dollar in international finance.[35]

These arguments against greater exchange-rate flexibility in the Common Market, just as many of the arguments used in the fixed-flexible exchange-rate controversy, however, compare the relative merits of permanently fixed exchange rates and of rate flexibility when the actual choice is between adjustable pegs and greater flexibility in exchange rates. At the same time, the experience of the Common Market in recent years, as well as a consideration of the possible consequences of its enlargement, point to the conclusion that exchange-rate changes may not be a rare occurence.[36]

Accordingly, the arguments on the relative merits of alternative monetary arrangements need to be rephrased by making a distinction between changes in nominal and in real exchange rates. In the following, the former will be taken to be identical to changes in official exchange

[35] The following is a representative statement on the alleged disadvantages of greater exchange-rate flexibility in the Common Market:

"Such an arrangement would have serious disadvantages. It would of its nature tend to make for divergence, rather than the desired convergence, in the development of the economies. It would prevent the adjustments normally made by trade flows between the member countries, which enable situations of temporary divergence to be brought under control under normal conditions. It would be very liable to impede the optimum orientation of capital flows within the community. It would have adverse effects socially, especially for immigrant workers. And psychologically it would be highly prejudicial to the confidence in the Common Market currencies that is necessary if the community is to work as it should and to function as a centre of stability", A Plan for an Economic and Monetary Union, *op. cit.*, p. 6.

[36] Cf. Sections I and II above.

rates while the latter will express changes in nominal rates adjusted for relative price changes.[37]

Official exchange rates should be understood in relative terms, *i.e.* in their relationship to the currencies of other countries rather than in terms of gold.[38] This necessitates the choice of a weighting scheme for averaging parity changes in foreign countries. Excluding from our purview the non-trade items of the balance of payments, weighting by the value of exports and imports seems appropriate. The same weighting scheme should be used in averaging domestic and foreign prices to calculate changes in real exchange rates.[39]

The question is then if economic agents react to changes in nominal or in real exchange rates. This question will be considered in regard to trade, domestic investment, direct foreign investment, portfolio investment, labor movements and speculation in foreign-exchange markets. Attention will further be given to the policy implications of rate flexibility.

Adjustable Peg or Rate-Flexibility

An oft-invoked argument against exchange-rate flexibility is the uncertainty it creates in foreign trade. While the usual response to this objection is that traders can cover the exchange risk on the forward market, it is in turn argued that forward exchange operations are costly and that they cannot be used to fully cover the exchange risk when the period of production for export markets is relatively long.

Let me start with the case when production is instantaneous or exports take place from stocks and payment is made by using a time bill. There will now be an exchange risk also under the system of adjustable pegs and, while the probability of a change in the exchange rate will on the average be smaller than under freely floating rates, the amplitude of changes will be larger. At the same time, the experience of Canada during the periods 1950-1962 indicates that freely fluctuating rates do not

[37] This distinction was introduced in my "Regional Monetary Integration of the Developing Countries: Comment", in Robert A. Mundell and Alexander K. Swoboda (eds.), *Monetary Problems of the International Economy,* Chicago, University of Chicago Press, 1969; pp. 151-156.

[38] A country's official exchange rate adjusted for changes in the exchange rates of its trading partners has been called the effective exchange rate. Cf. Fred Hirsch and Ilse Higgins, "An Indicator of Effective Exchange Rates", *International Monetary Fund Staff Papers,* November 1970; pp. 653-687.

[39] For certain purposes, one may wish to derive two indices of real exchange rates also, one for exports and one for imports. However, these and other practical problems of deriving the indices fall outside the scope of this paper.

discourage trade and that the cost of forward cover is relatively small. This will certainly be the case under orderly exchange markets ; in contrast, the cost of the forward cover is high for an overvalued currency and the crises associated with changes in parities tend to make obtaining forward cover difficult if not impossible. Still, on this count, the system of crawling pegs is superior to the other two alternatives as small movements in parities may not even make it necessary to cover the exchange risk.

I come next to the case when the production period is long. It should be apparent that in this event changes in the real exchange rate rather than in the nominal rate will be relevant for the exporter. This is because profitability will depend both on changes in the nominal rate and in the domestic prices of inputs.

In the adjustable peg system, the cumulated change in the real exchange rate due to domestic price changes will now be intermittently offset—or more than offset—by discontinuous changes in the nominal exchange rate. Thus, in a country where domestic prices are rising more rapidly than elsewhere, the profitability of exports will decline until a devaluation takes place which will abruptly bring a substantial improvement. The resulting fluctuations in the real exchange rate will in turn create uncertainty in decisions on production and trade.

Although under freely floating exchange rates, disparate changes in prices tend to be compensated by changes in nominal exchange rates, nonrecurrent capital movements and other transactions—including speculation in foreign-exchange markets—may nevertheless lead to fluctuations in the real exchange rate. This will not be the case, and real exchange rates will remain constant,[40] in a crawling-peg system, provided that variations in relative prices do not exceed the amount of allowed exchange-rate fluctuations. In such an event, then, the element of uncertainty due to changes in real exchange rates will be practically eliminated.

These considerations apply to trade in manufactured goods as well as in agricultural products. The latter is of especial interest as it has been repeatedly argued that the maintenance of fixed exchange rates is a *sine qua non* of the common agricultural policy, under which agricultural prices are fixed at identical levels for the entire Community. But the profitability of agriculture is also affected by changes in the prices of domestic products which are used as inputs or are consumed by the farmer, so that differing trends in these prices create disparities in farmers' real incomes in the member countries. And while freely floating

---

[40] I assume here for simplicity that the constancy of real exchanges rates is necessary to maintain balance-of-payments equilibrium. Should this instead require continuous changes in the real exchange rates, the above discussion can be reinterpreted in terms of fluctuations around a trend.

exchange rates will create uncertainty for the farmer, a system of crawling pegs can ensure the parallel movement of the prices he pays and receives.

Domestic investment in facilities destined for selling both at home and abroad or competing with imports also requires the constancy of real exchange rates. This will ensure parallel changes in the profitability of domestic and foreign sales and will eliminate uncertainty in investment decisions that are due to fluctuations in real exchange rates. Rather than providing a framework of certainty for investment decisions relating to exports and imports, however, a system of adjustable pegs creates uncertainty for these decisions by giving rise to fluctuations in real exchange rates. Short-term fluctuations in real exchange rates in a system of freely flexible rates are much less of a problem for investment decisions that necessarily involve a long time horizon and, as we have seen, there are no such fluctuations under the crawling peg.

Direct foreign investment, too, tends to be discouraged if real exchange rates fluctuate over time because of uncertainty in regard to both the relative competitiveness of foreign installations and the domestic currency value of repatriated earnings. Also, under the adjustable peg system, foreign investment may respond to existing exchange rates that are under- or overvalued to varying degrees, thus leading to an inefficient allocation of world resources. The incentives provided by the overvaluation of the U.S. dollar to American investments in Western Europe during the sixties is a case in point.

These conclusions also apply to labor migration. Variations in real exchange rates create uncertainty with respect to intercountry differences in real wages and the domestic currency value of remittances from abroad. There might also be excess inward and outward migration which involves an economic as well as a social cost.

Decisions on the purchase of foreign stocks will be influenced by changes in the real as well as in the nominal exchange rate. For one thing, stock prices tend to vary with the profitability of foreign companies, which is affected by changes in the real exchange rate; for another, changes in the nominal rate will affect the timing of sales and purchases. The efficient allocation of investment funds and the avoidance of uncertainty thus call for constancy in real exchange rates.

In turn, the purchase and sale of fixed income obligations is affected only by changes in nominal exchange rates. In the case of non-transferable long-term obligations, there is an exchange risk irrespective of whether exchange rates change in a continuous or a discontinuous fashion. For transferable long-term obligations, however, the exchange risk is reduced if rate flexibility is introduced. But this leads us to the question of speculation on the foreign-exchange market which might take the form of transactions in long-term or short-term securities or in foreign currency.

It has often been argued that freely fluctuating exchange rates may have a destabilizing influence giving rise to large movements in rates that are not warranted by the underlying economic conditions. A more sophisticated form of this argument is that speculators can prove themselves right as the depreciation in the exchange rate resulting from speculative sales leads to higher domestic costs through increases in the prices of imported inputs and wage goods. Now, as wage increases are not reversible, a permanent rise in the domestic cost and price level will ensue, warranting the depreciation of the exchange rate.

While I find it difficult to accept the view that speculators would have a long enough time horizon to anticipate wage and price increases due to the inflationary effects of a depreciation of the exchange rate, the possibility of destabilizing speculation under freely floating exchange rates cannot be excluded. It should be added, however, that there is no evidence of destabilizing speculation for the periods when Canada has applied freely floating exchange rates ; rather, short-term capital flows appear to have had a stabilizing influence.[41]

By contrast, the foreign-exchange crises of recent years have given rise to substantial speculative activity which in several instances appears to have triggered the decision to change the parity or to float the rate. Such one-way speculation is practically riskless and successful speculators make profits at the expense of central banks that intervene in the foreign-exchange market to maintain the rate within predetermined limits. From available information, it appears that in 1967 the Bank of England lost over $130 million by selling U.S. dollars before, and repurchasing them after, the devaluation of the pound.[42] Even larger profits were made by speculators on the occasion of the foreign-exchange crises of 1969 and 1971.

This situation reflects the fact that the amount of funds made available for speculation has increased to a considerable extent during the last decade. The participants include—apart from "professional" speculators—investors and traders as well as multinational corporations and even some central banks who want to avoid capital losses due to exchange-rate changes or who wish to make a profit. In effect, we observe a "learning process", with many new entrants in the game at every new crisis.

---

[41] Cf. *e.g.* Thomas L. Powrie, "Short-term Capital Movements and the Flexible Exchange Rate, 1953-1961", *Canadian Journal of Economics and Political Science,* February 1964.

[42] Cf. Robert M. Dunn, Jr., "International Payment Adjustment Problems Arising from Economic Integration", in *U.S. Foreign Economic Policy for the 1970s : A New Approach to New Realities,* Washington, National Planning Association, 1971, p. 146.

period is largely explained by the ability and willingness of the two major deficit countries—the United States and the United Kingdom—to deal with their balance-of-payments problems without a devaluation. Its central position in the world economy as well as the use of the dollar as a reserve currency and as a means of payment in international trade and in capital markets enabled the United States to increase its foreign liabilities from $7 billion in 1949 to over $50 billion in 1971. In turn, the United Kingdom applied stop-and-go policies for a protracted period in order to avoid the devaluation of the pound.

The reluctance of foreign countries to continue accumulating dollars practically eliminates the possibility of increasing the dollar liabilities of the United States, and the U.S. is not prepared to sacrifice domestic objectives for the sake of balance-of-payments equilibrium. Nor does the United Kingdom appear willing any longer to accept slower growth resulting from the intermittent application of deflationary policies as a price of maintaining the parity of the pound. And should countries other than the United States and the United Kingdom incur deficits in the future, they too seem to be reluctant to place the brunt of the adjustment on the domestic economy. In turn, in the case of Germany, we observe a reluctance to import inflation by maintaining fixed parities.

With the sluggishness in the adjustment process under fixed exchange rates, then, balance-of-payments disequilibria are bound to occur and can be expected to engender speculation that will further aggravate the situation. At the same time, it is doubtful that a widening of margins by itself would be an appropriate remedy. On the one hand, this allows considerable short-term flexibility, thereby giving rise to fluctuations in real exchange rates and hence uncertainty in foreign trade ; on the other hand, there is no provision for long-term flexibility so that, in the presence of divergent price trends, currencies may soon reach their floor or ceiling.[45]

In the face of the possible occurrence of disequilibria among Common Market currencies, it has been suggested that these countries undertake relatively small exchange-rate changes of 4-5 per cent to remedy eventual disequilibria. It is difficult to see how this method could be applied in practice. Apart from the problems involved in determining at what point a parity change of 4-5 per cent becomes necessary, we observe a tendency on the part of governments to postpone a change in parity as long as

---

[45] As Fred Hirsch expressed it : "The wider band system ... risks of being either too rigid or too volatile. It may have a double disadvantage. It gives perhaps excessive immediate flexibility [and] involves significant uncertainty to traders and investors. At the same time ... it has inadequate continuing flexibility." Fred Hirsch, *Money International,* London, Penguin Press, 1969 ; p. 432.

possible in the hope that it can in the end be avoided. It also appears that governments prefer to incur the opprobrium associated with larger parity changes at greater intervals to smaller changes carried out more often. Moreover, following the French example, a devaluing country may use the occasion of a balance-of-payments deficit to overdevalue in order to obtain a competitive advantage, or it may apply exchange restrictions in lieu of a devaluation.

IV. POLICY IMPLICATIONS AND CONCLUSIONS

Arguments against the Crawling Peg

The above considerations point to the desirability for the European Common Market of adopting a system of crawling pegs in preference to adjustable pegs or freely fluctuating exchange rates. But there are several objections to the crawling peg that need to be dealt with. First of all, there is the practical question of whether crawling pegs would have remedied balance-of-payments disequilibria in the past, and whether the margin of manoeuvre provided by crawling pegs is sufficient to handle disequilibria that may be expected in the future. A related question is whether the "discipline" imposed by fixed rates will be removed by the introduction of limited exchange-rate flexibility, thereby reducing resistance to inflationary pressures and thus engendering disequilibria which a system of limited flexibility cannot handle. Finally, the objection has been put forward that the increased freedom of domestic policies associated with the possibility for exchange-rate variations would hurt efforts made for economic and political integration in the Common Market and, at the same time, confirm the central role of the dollar.

As regards the first question, it is not sufficient to limit our attention to cases when parity changes have eventually occurred but we should also consider instances when domestic measures were used to avert a parity change at a cost to the national economy. Among the present member countries of the EEC, such was the case in Italy in the years 1963-1964 when severe deflationary measures were applied to avoid a devaluation. But the classic case is that of the United Kingdom whose economic growth over much of the fifties and the sixties was adversely affected by the application of stop-and-go policies for the sake of avoiding a devaluation of the pound. Restrictive policies periodically cut short an incipient investment boom, thereby leading to a reduction in the rate of investment and the rate of economic growth. These results could have been avoided in a system of crawling pegs which also would have obviated the need for the imposition of the import surcharge in 1964 and the devaluation of 1967. In this connection, one may note that the devaluation of 14.3 per cent undertaken in November 1967 was equivalent to an annual exchange-rate change of 2 per cent over a seven-year period.

Similar considerations apply to the German revaluations of 5 per cent in 1962 and 8.5 per cent in 1969. Both of these revaluations followed a long period of surplus that was artificially limited by inducements provided to export capital. The application of crawling pegs would have checked the cumulative process which took the form of export increases leading to investment in new facilities, reductions in domestic costs and, again, increases in exports.[46]

The question is more difficult to answer in regard to the situation in France in 1968-1969. The May events in 1968 led to a rapid reversal of the French balance-of-payments situation, entailing a fall in reserves by about one-half within a year, notwithstanding the application of payments restrictions. The extent of speculative flows contributing to the reserve loss, as well as the size of the wage settlement of the summer of 1968, may have been smaller, however, if the French were committed not to devalue beyond the "crawl". At the same time, as noted above, the 12.5 per cent devaluation was excessive ; between the first quarter of 1968 and the second quarter of 1969 French industrial prices rose 9 per cent and industrial wages 14 per cent as compared to average increases of 4 and 9 per cent in France's major trading partners.[47] If we also consider that the French franc was at its ceiling before the May events, crawling pegs together with a movement of the rate within the margin of permissible exchange-rate fluctuations could have sufficed to maintain equilibrium in the French balance of payments.

Finally, in the case of the U.S. dollar and the Japanese yen, imbalances developed over a long time period and both countries applied a variety of measures to avoid a change in parity. These measures created distortions in trade and capital movements and they could have been obviated, and subsequent exchange-rate adjustments avoided, if crawling pegs had been applied.

To consider imbalances in a national context is, however, a partial exercise. Rather, emphasis should be put on changes in the exchange rates of all the major trading nations since, for any particular country, the relationship of its exchange rate to that of its trading partners is relevant. With exchange rates changing in different directions at different rates

[46] Cf. W. Beckerman, "Projecting Europe's Growth", *Economic Journal,* Vol. 72, December 1962 ; pp. 912-925, and the controversy between Bela Balassa and W. Beckerman in *Economic Journal,* Vol. 74, December 1963 ; pp. 781-789 and Vol. 74, March and September 1964 ; pp. 240-242 and pp. 738-742, respectively.

[47] *International Financial Statistics,* December 1971 - Averages have been calculated by weighting with the sum of exports and imports in trade with France.

within the limit of annual changes of 2 per cent under a system of crawling pegs, one may avoid "fundamental disequilibria" from developing. In particular, the flexibility provided by this system appears large enough to take care of differences in the "transformation" and "preference" functions among the Common Market countries. Data for the past ten years, as well as projections for the period 1971-1975, do not show a divergence in the rate of increase of prices that could not be handled with a 2 per cent crawl.

But how about the objection that introducing the crawling peg would weaken the determination of governments to restrain inflation, thereby widening the gap in price trends between countries ? There is a two-fold answer to this question. First, in the deficit countries a depreciating exchange rate may have a greater restraining effect on inflationary policies than the loss of reserves under the fixed exchange rate system. A major reason is that the depreciation of the rate is immediately apparent while reserve losses can be disguised, at least temporarily.

Second, the institution of limited exchange-rate flexibility may be accompanied by a more credible commitment to forego a devaluation, thereby restraining inflationary expectations. Governments will find it easier to accept, and to adhere to, a less rigid obligation that provides a safety valve in the form of a possible depreciation or appreciation of 2 per cent a year. In turn, entrepreneurs may offer greater resistance to outsized wage increases if the likelihood of changes in fixed parities is reduced.

I come finally to the effects of a system of crawling pegs on the process of European integration. The critics maintain that, by providing greater possibilities for policy differences, the application of crawling pegs would give less of an incentive for policy coordination in the framework of the EEC than does the present system of adjustable pegs. The events of recent years seem to indicate, however, that rather than being conducive to policy coordination, the present system has led to a policy-coordination-cycle from crisis to a declaration of good intentions on policy coordination to crisis again. And, apart from repeatedly bringing to a halt efforts made to coordinate monetary and fiscal policies, the recurring crises have interfered with the operation of the common agricultural policy and the coordination of other policies.

Every parity change led to temporizing and stop-gap measures in agriculture, aimed at offsetting the effects of exchange-rate changes on agricultural prices and/or incomes. Following the August 1969 devaluation, France adopted a tax-subsidy scheme for a period of two years to avoid increases in agricultural prices. In turn, German farmers were compensated in the form of deficiency payments for the decline in farm prices associated with the October 1969 revaluation of the mark. Finally, tax-subsidy schemes were imposed in 1971, and were continued after the setting of new parities, thereby insulating national markets in agricultural products from the effects of changes in exchange rates.[48]

In devaluing countries, the use of tax-subsidy measures reflect the desire of governments to escape cost-push inflation resulting from higher food prices ; in revaluing countries they indicate the political power of farmer interests that wish to avoid losing the advantages gained through favorable developments in industrial prices. At the same time, these measures have created distortions in intra-EEC trade in agricultural products as well as in resource allocation between agriculture and industry in each of the member countries.

In focusing attention on problems raised by exchange-rate changes, the system of adjustable pegs has also contributed to postponing the reform of the common agricultural policy of the EEC. Furthermore, it has made agreements difficult in areas, such as transportation, where parity changes affect the competitive position of national industries. Finally, the concentration of energies on monetary integration, and the failure of these efforts, have adversely affected policy coordination in other areas.

To begin with the latter point, the setbacks of efforts for monetary integration have created a certain pessimism both within and outside the Commission concerning the future prospects for European integration. Also, given the limitations on the Commission's capacity to raise and pursue matters relating to integration, as well as limitations on the possibilities of national governments and the public to entertain such propositions in several areas simultaneously, the emphasis on monetary questions has made it difficult to pursue integration efforts in areas such as technological and regional policies.

Limited Flexibility and Policy Coordination

I submit that policy coordination in the European Common Market has greater chances for success if limited flexibility in exchange rates is admitted. To begin with, in adopting a system of crawling pegs, one can avoid disparate changes in the probability of agriculture in the member countries that result from differential rates of price increases of industrial products purchased by the farmer and can forego the crises in the common agricultural policy that invariably occur at the time of changes in exchange parities. Member countries may also be more willing to accept new commitments for policy harmonization in areas such as direct and

[48] Tax-subsidy schemes involve taxing (subsidizing) agricultural imports and subsidizing (taxing) agricultural exports in revaluing (devaluing) countries.

indirect taxation, transport and energy policy, and technological policy if the constancy of real exchange rates is assured. More generally, as a bone of contention—adjustments in the peg—is removed, it should be easier to reach agreements on policy objectives and on the use of policy instruments.

As far as the exchange rate is concerned, policy coordination may take the form of agreeing on the direction of the "crawl" by the currencies of the individual Common Market countries. Eventually, central banks may aim at a joint crawl, with provisions for continuing flexibility in the event that one of the currencies is at the ceiling, or at the floor, of the band of permissible exchange-rate variations.

In turn, the band of permissible exchange-rate variations among Common Market currencies would need to be narrowed. Under the present system non-recurrent flows, such as temporary short-term capital movements, give rise to fluctuations in nominal as well as in real exchange rates. Such fluctuations create uncertainty in intra-EEC trade, interfere with the establishment of a European capital market, and discourage the use of Common Market currencies for purposes of intervention in foreign exchange markets.

Having eliminated barriers to trade and, in part, to factor movements and aiming at greater integration of their national economies, the EEC countries should adopt a narrower band of exchange-rate variations among their currencies than vis-à-vis the currencies of non-member countries. This compares to the present situation when the permissible range of exchange-rate variations among Common Market currencies is double that vis-à-vis the U.S. dollar.[49]

Agreements on the crawl and a narrowing of the band would also necessitate the increased cooperation of central banks in intervening in foreign-exchange markets so as to support decisions taken on the crawl and to smooth out fluctuations due to non-recurring changes without nevertheless attempting to move against the trend. The system envisaged here is thus discretionary rather than automatic but it should be responsive to market signals.

While interventions in foreign-exchange markets could initially be carried out by central banks, it appears desirable that this be done by a foreign-exchange stabilization fund which would also provide short-term credits. The establishment of such a fund is presently unacceptable to Germany which considers itself a potential creditor. The institution of crawling pegs would obviate these fears and permit the fund's establish-

[49] The reason is that margins are defined with respect to the U.S. dollar and two Common Market currencies may find themselves at opposite ends of the band in relation to the dollar.

inefficiencies in resource allocation can be reduced if fluctuations in real exchange rates are avoided. This, in turn, can be accomplished by adopting a system of crawling pegs. The conclusion is reinforced if we consider the process of decision-making on parity changes which creates a tendency to postpone such changes, involves explicit or implicit bargaining, and gives rise to speculation.

I have further suggested that the adoption of a system of crawling pegs be accompanied by narrowing the margins of permissible fluctuations among Common Market currencies, establishing an exchange stabilization fund, and creating a common currency unit. Narrowing of the margins would reduce uncertainty in intra-EEC transactions ; the stabilization fund would provide short-term loans and carry out interventions in foreign-exchange markets ; while the new unit would assume functions presently fulfilled by national currencies and the U.S. dollar.

These recommendations would entail approaching the goal of economic and monetary integration by creating the conditions for such an outcome rather than attempting to force the premature establishment of fixed parities that tends to exacerbate the conflict of national interests. In this way, it can be hoped that progress may be made without the periodical crises of the past.

A Comment on European Monetary Integration 8

Herman R. WORTMANN
Commission of the European Communities

My reflections on the papers presented by Bela Balassa, Harry Johnson and Robert Triffin can be organized around three different themes or problem areas : (*a*) the Doctrine of Parallelism ; (*b*) Towards intra-EEC Flexibility ? and (*c*) Will Regional Adjustment be Insufficient without Political Integration ?

THE DOCTRINE OF PARALLELISM

(1) Member States remain for some time to come exposed to national factors and pressures—economic, political, social ones ; short-term economic situations and cyclical behaviour will therefore be different in the individual countries. These differences—instead of being judged as a positive sign, permitting countries to follow, to some (*i.e.* cyclical) extent, national trends according to national requirements—will time and again be interpreted as failures to reach effective coordination in economic policy objectives and economic development. Such an interpretation would be incorrect and would, in any case, raise doubt as to the credibility of any plan towards economic and monetary union.

(2) The Werner Plan stressed the principle of parallelism : simultaneous progress in the field of coordination of economic policy and of monetary cooperation. In the light of the events in the past year, is this principle correct and operational ?

(3) Threats coming from outside, together with doubts coming from inside, tend to put the question boldly in terms of political courage and challenge. Do we want to organize the economics of full integration, together with its political implications or not ?

If we open our economies up to the point where we can no longer shelter ourselves against influences from our neighbours—and are not willing to do so—we must expect the greater likelihood of disequilibria among members and regard them as problems of the Community as a whole. In other words, intra-Community imbalances are to a large extent not obstacles to but consequences of integration. These imbalances are unavoidable and should be treated differently from ordinary balance-of-payments disequilibria.

(4) It has been said that the "economic school of thought" is more fundamental to further European integration than the "monetary school of thought" but that the latter is more operational. In particular, the idea of an exchange-rate system proper to Europe within the world-wide system (known as the snake in the tunnel) has the great virtue of putting the central banks practically into business. They have to run this system and make a success out of it. They will have interest in "real" coordination of policies, lest the snake collapses as soon as EEC currencies find themselves too often at opposite sides of it. It is true that a more careful study of the functioning of such a system reveals a substantial number of problems, the nature of which appears not to be of a technical, pragmatic character but of a fundamental, conceptual one—but they are not at all impossible to solve. These problems are : how does one operate a Community "snake" in a Community "tunnel" and how does one move the "snake" up and down as long as one has national concepts of balance-of-payments objectives, different balance-of-payments structures, national concepts of the role that exchange-rate policy has to play and as long as one has profoundly divergent opinions as to the appropriate mix between exchange-rate flexibility and exchange controls, which are, to some extent, alternatives ? What is to be done when no satisfactory procedures can be worked out concerning the movement of the "snake", concerning currencies that stick to the limit, concerning intervention in non-convertible dollars, etc. ? Has not the discussion on flexibility and crawling pegs led to the conclusion by most monetary authorities that there are no satisfactory automatic mechanisms that can serve as a "hidden hand" for guiding the exchange rate ? If this is so, judgment must come in at frequent intervals and we must therefore organize and improve the decision-making process in this field of exchange-rate policy coordination. Member countries of the Community have not been able in 1971 to agree on any alternative to dispersed floating and the Community has constantly been faced with the problem of finding mechanisms for common action against a common cause of trouble. I am convinced that 1972 will show a very substantial "qualitative jump" in the procedures of coordination and that the necessary reform of the international monetary system will not take place if Europe is not able to organize its own exchange-rate system.

(5) As could be expected, more than one author has expressed sympathy for the idea of more flexibility within the Community, be it in the form of crawling pegs, flexible exchange rates or wider bands. Experience with the adjustable peg has indeed not been too successful. I consider this, however, more a matter of bad application of the right principles (adjustable peg) than as a logical consequence of the correct application of bad principles. Have not most difficulties been the consequence of the fact that governments have only decided to change parities once inappropriateness has become so glaring as to require a major change ? This is why speculative capital movements have disturbed the smooth functioning of the system, which becomes particularly dangerous when the parity of a reserve currency has moved out of line.

As to the crawling peg, powerful arguments have been developed by Balassa, who has submitted the statement that this system is not only compatible with European integration but would even increase the chance of success of policy coordination. However this may be, this idea has many opponents who are no less brilliant than Professor Balassa (Kindleberger, Triffin, etc.). They object to the idea, implicit in the case for flexible exchange rates, that the external equilibrium which comes from allowing equality of supply and demand for foreign exchange is an equilibrium not only for the balance of payments but also for prices, wages, employment, etc. As a matter of fact, the free rate may clear the foreign-exchange market but not the labor market or the market for goods and services. One should furthermore consider that intra-Community flexibility also removes the need for harmonization. Finally, it seems of practical importance to note that considerable resistance has arisen in recent years as to any *automatic formula* version of the crawling peg. This being the case, parity changes remain determined by men, who can or cannot make up their minds as to the appropriateness and timing of parity changes. We are therefore back to the problem of how to assure adjustment of parities once and as soon as they become unrealistic. Triffin has repeated his suggestion to empower the IMF to exert pressure on a member State who should modify its parity but cannot bring itself to do so. I would agree with Triffin's idea of making exchange-rate changes *compulsory* in certain situations.

(6) Different opinions have been expressed as to the desirable mix of *flexibility on the one hand, controls on the other.* Triffin has mentioned the two-tier exchange system without seeming to be much in favour of it. He proposes rather to cope with disturbing capital movements by setting up a broad network of multilateralized swap agreements. Balassa and Johnson rely more on exchange-rate flexibility but one may ask whether

some form of exchange control would not appear necessary in a world that is becoming smaller and smaller and where a number of factors are responsible for a spectacular growth of liquid funds susceptible to be moved out of one currency and into another according to circumstances. The question arises whether the European Community can have capital controls that differ widely from one country to the other. Individual countries have indeed developed over the past years an impressive number of instruments capable to some extent to cope with those capital movements but they have been designed and adopted on a purely national basis (regulation of deposits of non-residents, minimum reserve requirements, regulation of borrowing abroad, regulation of net foreign position of banks, double exchange markets and outright exchange controls).

If the European Community would like to impress its own personality on the international monetary system, it should have not only its own exchange-rate system but also a common system of control over disruptive capital flows. What should be the common denominator of the instruments that could permit to develop smoothly but rapidly a common or concerted European policy in this matter ? I note that none of the authors have approached the problem from this angle.

WILL REGIONAL ADJUSTMENTS BE INSUFFICIENT WITHOUT POLITICAL INTEGRATON ?

(7) Balassa's consideration of the functioning of the regional adjustment process, assuring adjustment between regions of a large monetary area such as the U.S.A., by automatic stabilizers as well as by discretionary measures to support depressed regions brings him to doubt the possibility of reaching immutably fixed exchange rates within the Community before political integration has been achieved. It would be of interest to discuss this fundamental point in greater detail as the concept of "political integration" is a fairly vague one and could take different forms and different degrees of intensity. Could we say that autonomy is lost once we have to accept a given rate of inflation, even if this rate can be considered by international standards as not unreasonable ? And do we consider autonomy to be unaffected just because we consider our European countries of an appropriate size to organize our own economic life ?

As Professor Johnson has clearly pointed out, if the identification of nations with currency areas it questioned, it appears that no single criterion could be developed on purely economic considerations.

Mundell looks at mobility of factors, McKinnon at trade in goods and services, Kenen at diversity and flexibility and Haberler at the degree of similarity of policy objectives in relation with the trade-off between inflation and unemployment. It seems that for political and practical reasons the last concept is the most useful : the European Commission has therefore laid much emphasis on the problem of compatibility of policy objectives.

However this may be, I tend to take the view that a substantial degree of "political autonomy" can be maintained even if governments agree to

- make policy objectives compatible (as far as economics is concerned) ; more particularly, member countries should agree on a set of policy objectives that would not permit the pursuit of divergent monetary and fiscal policies which would inevitably result in payments imbalances ;
- develop a large mass of financial instruments acceptable in payments throughout the area. The greater the mass of private negotiable instruments the larger will be the scope for automatic adjustment between regions of the Community, the less stress will have to be laid on a deliberate regional policy and the smaller will be the adjustment to be made by central banks ; this implies in particular that national governments will be limited in their ability to finance budget deficits through domestic credit expansion, *i.e.* by the banking system ; they will have to rely instead on their capacity to raise funds by issuing securities in a Community-wide capital market. As a consequence, the funds drawn into the area in question would compensate for the deflationary pressures of a regional payments deficit. It is evident that such financing can only cope with regional imbalances which are of a temporary and reversible nature ; persistent weaknesses of regional areas should be coped with by deliberate structural policies. The Community should accept a common responsibility for depressed areas, improve the mobility of labour and strengthen the infra-structure of these regions ;
- introduce a Community-financed unemployment compensation as a means to redistribute purchasing power according to changes in economic activity and in employment levels ;
- develop a new European currency to supplement existing ones and to take over gradually some of the functions now exercised by the U.S. dollar (and foster its acceptance and attractiveness by special measures as has been suggested by Williamson and Magnifico) ;
- change intra-EEC parity relations more promptly during the transitional period, as soon as they become unrealistic (these changes could perhaps be made compulsory in certain situations).

The Problem of Disruptive International Capital Flows 9

J. Marcus FLEMING
International Monetary Fund

INTRODUCTION

Notoriously, there has been a substantial increase in recent years in the magnitude of temporary and reversible capital flows between countries. You have all heard figures quoted showing how, from one currency crisis to the next, an ever larger avalanche of funds passes out of—or more recently into—countries whose currencies are under pressure. We, in the International Monetary Fund, have tried to measure these things in a rather staid and statistical way. There are some thirteen countries, mostly industrial, for which we possess quarterly balance-of-payments statistics. For these thirteen countries, we have measured, over the eight-year period ending in December 1970, the quarterly deviations from trend in total capital flows (including errors and omissions). Having summed these up for all countries, irrespective of sign, we find that these aggregate deviations in capital flows grew over the eight-year period at an average rate of 21-22 per cent per annum, as against a growth of only 10 per cent per annum in the international trade of the same countries.

To a large extent these fluctuations in capital flows were accounted for by flows of short-term capital, but not entirely. Deviations from trend in the flow of short-term capital, which also grew in the aggregate by some 20 per cent per annum over the period, were on the average 10 per cent smaller than deviations in total capital flows.

These fluctuations in capital flows were not always disequilibrating in the sense of making payments imbalances larger than they would otherwise have been. Often they tended to reduce imbalances, especially in quiet times when, in any case, capital flows were relatively steady and payments imbalances relatively small. But more often these fluctuations were disequilibrating, especially when large, and especially in more recent years. Largely as a consequence of this fact, the quarterly payments imbalances of the countries in our sample, like the deviations in capital flows themselves, have risen over the eight years in question by something like 23.2 per cent per annum. It is with these disequilibrating capital flows that I am primarily concerned.

CAUSES OF DISEQUILIBRATING FLOWS

There is no mystery about why these disequilibrating flows occur, and why they have increased in importance. Sometimes such flows occur on account of changes in the relative profitability of investment in different parts of the world. A sustained movement of this kind affecting longer-term capital and direct investment as well as short-term funds took place from the United States to Europe in the early '60s, and similar movements have strongly affected the payments balances of Canada, Australia, and many other countries. More temporary and, therefore, more disturbing movements of profit- and interest-motivated capital have taken place as a result of differences in the phasing of the trade cycle in different countries. But the most important cause of disruptive capital flows, especially in recent years, is of course to be found in the emergence, from time to time, of expectations of imminent appreciation or depreciation of particular currencies. It is this factor that has been responsible for almost all the really large disturbances in payments balances.

The proximate causes for the great expansion in disequilibrating capital flows in recent years are to be found in the increasing frequency and likelihood of exchange-rate alterations, culminating in the virtual suspension of the par value system on 15 August of last year and in the increasing readiness of capital to move from country to country in response to any incentive. There is a certain circularity in the explanatory system, since the disequilibrating flows are themselves partly to blame for the instability of exchange rates. There are, however, underlying causes of the latter phenomenon on which it would be tempting to enlarge. Two of these are worth mentioning. One is the increased importance of the cost-push elements in inflation ; these make it much more difficult for governments to keep relative price levels and balances of payments in line than under the old type of demand-pull inflation. Another is the situation which has become particularly marked over the last few years whereby the United States, when in deficit, can generate reserves in the rest of the world without comparable loss to its own reserves ; this has exercised strong pressure towards exchange appreciation and revaluation.

The causes of the enhanced mobility of capital between countries are well known—the relaxation of capital controls in the '50s and early '60s, the spread of international business, and the provision of cheaper and more efficient intermediation through the Euro-currency and Euro-bond markets.

The effects of these volatile flows are as familiar as their causes and we need not dwell upon them. They not only keep central bankers awake at night, but also made it very difficult for countries to maintain monetary stability and to adhere to targets of demand policy. They enforce unwanted changes in exchange parities, give rise to "clean" or "dirty" floats, and they have even brought about, in the second half of 1971, a virtual breakdown in the par value system. Yet their effects are not always bad. Sometimes they speed up adjustments of relative price levels that have to take place if real resources are to flow throughout the world to the places where they can be most usefully employed. This, of course, is what has been happening recently between the United States and some other industrial countries.

REMEDIAL MEASURES

Let us, however, assume that the system has a tendency to generate disequilibrating capital flows on an excessive scale and often in inappropriate circumstances. What measures can governments take to restrain them or rob them of their disturbing effects? In a word, they can offset them domestically, they can finance them internationally, they can control them, and they can adjust the current account to accommodate them.

Governments can seek to offset the domestic effects of disequilibrating capital flows on the money base, on the supply of money, on interest rates, and on the demand for goods and services.

They may offset the external effects of these private international flows—the effects on their own reserves or on those of other countries—by official international borrowing or lending, by varying central bank holdings of foreign exchange, by using inter-central bank swap arrangements, by lending or borrowing via the IMF, or the BIS, by official borrowing on the private market, by governmental lending or advance repayment of loans outside the central bank.

The controlling or influencing of private capital flows can take a wide variety of forms, each of which merits extensive treatment. There is the use of internationally oriented interest-rate policy, accompanied or not accompanied by fiscal or monetary measures to compensate the domestic effects. There are policies involving the direct quantitative restriction or promotion of capital flows. Some of these regulate external positions or foreign-exchange positions, others relate to transactions. Some are confined to banks and similar financial institutions, others extend to other firms and to individuals. There are also fiscal measures directly affecting foreign investment or the income from it.

Finally, recourse can be had to an important set of possible policies affecting exchange-market intervention. First, there is the possibility of official intervention in the forward-exchange market. Second, a system of dual exchange rates for capital and current transactions can be applied.

And third, there is the radical remedy of permitting, with or without limits, flexibility in the spot exchange rate.

This last policy, though primarily designed to choke off disturbing capital flows, may also be said to implement or accommodate them insofar as it tends to adapt the current account balance of payments to changes in the capital account.

There is thus a vast, even a bewildering array of measures that can be adopted to deal with disruptive capital flows. Are any lessons to be drawn from experience as to their effectiveness and relative merits in different situations ?

MONETARY OFFSETTING

The technique of monetary offsetting is carried out by means of open-market operations on the part of monetary authorities or public debt authorities, discount policy, variations in bank reserve requirements and similar measures, and direct control of bank credit. While normally successful, within limits, in preventing temporary capital flows from disturbing the domestic economy, such measures do nothing to stabilize the balance of payments or reserves. Indeed, since they thwart the limiting effect which interest-rate reactions would otherwise exercise on disturbing capital flows, they rely essentially on such flows being reversible, limited and temporary. No doubt they are—but the limits may be very wide if the flows, through their effects on reserve movements, are psychologically self-inflammatory. A country in deficit that relies on offsetting alone is apt to run out of reserves, and a country in substantial surplus that relies on this policy alone is apt to run short of domestic assets. A world that relied on offsetting and reserve movements alone would require a volume of reserves to meet its payments disequilibria that would be excessive from other points of view. Offsetting is, however, an essential element in any satisfactory policy mix for dealing with disturbing capital flows, and in many countries there is scope for improving the techniques of offsetting, which, to be successful, require a close cooperation of monetary and public debt authorities.

INTERNATIONAL FINANCING

Some of the deficiencies of mere offsetting as a means of dealing with disturbing capital flows can be remedied if it is complemented by arrangements for official international lending and borrowing. Lending by monetary authorities makes it possible for deficit countries to finance their deficits without reserve losses, and thus to continue their domestic offsetting policies. The deficits of reserve centers, for example, may be financed by additions to foreign-exchange holdings, those of other countries by the use of bilateral credit arrangements or by drawings on the Fund. Such policies, however, will do nothing to mitigate the reserve increases of surplus countries, and they lead to not wholly justifiable fluctuations in the stock of world reserves. More attention should perhaps be paid to the possibilities of official borrowing by deficit countries from the private market or from non-monetary public authorities in surplus countries. These will not merely moderate the reserve losses of the deficit countries but also the reserve gains of the surplus countries, and hence the fluctuations in world reserves, and will lighten the task of offsetting in both sets of countries. The borrowing by the Exim-Bank in the Euro-dollar market in the spring of last year was an example of what is wanted though probably less effective than U.S. borrowing in domestic capital markets would have been. Such acts of official financing, however, would have to be on a very large scale to offset the flows of private funds.

Thus far we have been considering techniques whereby the capital account has been adjusted to fit the current account, despite the existence of disequilibrating private capital flows, by official compensatory financing. We have now to consider techniques whereby private capital flows are themselves influenced in such a way as to promote the financing of the current account, despite the existence of autonomous disequilibrating tendencies.

INTERNATIONALLY ORIENTED INTEREST-RATE POLICIES

The time-honored method of achieving this result is to apply monetary or interest-rate policy to the preservation of external rather than domestic stability. In its more modern variant, monetary policy is relieved of its role in stabilizing the domestic economy through the assumption of that task by fiscal policy. This combination of policies can hardly hope to be effective in dealing with speculative capital flows —its role is necessarily confined to dealing with interest-motivated flows such as arise from national differences in the phasing of prosperity and recession. For this purpose it has, on the one hand, the advantage over other techniques that it makes use of familiar and well-tried policy instruments and that it operates even-handedly as between domestic and foreign capital flows and as among various types of capital flows, at any rate on short term. On the other hand, owing to the difficulty of maintaining a flexible governmental control over fiscal policy, it carries considerable dangers of reducing the effectiveness of demand management. Moreover, unless the accompanying fiscal measures are very specifically chosen to offset the effects of interest changes on expenditure, the fiscal/

monetary mix may lead to distortion in the proportion of national income that is saved and invested and maladjustment in the relative demand for the products of different industries.

DIRECT CAPITAL CONTROLS

If interest-rate policy is the classic liberal method of influencing capital flows, direct and more or less quantitative controls have been the almost equally classic illiberal method of doing so. Though traditionally used to restrict outpayments, they have of recent years been applied as much to the restriction of inpayments. It is important to distinguish two variants of this approach. One, the more modern variant, proceeds by regulating the assets and liabilities of banks, other financial institutions, and sometimes even large non-financial firms. The other proceeds by way of a regulation of individual foreign transactions. The former variant, which has been applied even by countries of a very liberal persuasion, usually involves setting maxima or minima to the net foreign positions or net foreign-exchange positions of the banks, etc. But sometimes gross positions, foreign assets or liabilities to foreigners are limited, or discouraged by differential reserve requirements, prohibition of interest, and the like. This type of regulation is relatively simple, and within its limits effective in dealing with flows of short-term money, but it is necessarily partial and may be bypassed by direct transactions of non-banks with the outside world. To make capital controls watertight requires a comprehensive system of surveillance over transactions on current as well as on capital account. Such a system, operating through individual licencing, is necessarily complicated, arbitrary and uneven in its incidence as among different types of capital flows. Moreover, it is, on balance, restrictive and irrational in that it fails to promote capital flows in one direction as much as it discourages them in the opposite direction. With all this, it is almost bound to leave important gaps and loopholes for evasion, particularly as regards trade credit, bank note transactions, intra-firm transfers, and the repatriation of capital generally. Banking regulations of the type described earlier may be very useful in the short run to meet sudden speculative attacks but comprehensive restrictions as a more permanent instrument for disciplining capital flows are unlikely to have much appeal to economists except in the streamlined modern form which I shall discuss in a moment, namely, the establishment of a separate exchange market for capital transactions.

FORWARD EXCHANGE INTERVENTION

We come now to several rather sophisticated ways of dealing with disruptive capital flows, all of them involving the exchange-rate system in one way or another. Official forward-exchange market intervention has been employed on a large scale in recent years as a way of moving interest-arbitrage funds in a direction counter to the current trend. Though its effects are largely confined to short-term funds it has the merit of affecting trade credit as well as bank credit and of impinging upon both outward and inward flows, discouraging one and encouraging the other. However, its flexibility and secrecy make it a very useful instrument for dealing with exchange-speculative capital flows, provided that these are of a genuinely temporary character. Since, however, official forward speculation will evoke a certain amount of private counter-speculation through its effect on the forward rate, forward-market intervention has less effect on the balance of payments than an equal amount of outright official lending or borrowing. This makes forward-market intervention rather an expensive way—for the monetary authorities—of postponing an exchange-rate adjustment.

DUAL EXCHANGE RATES

The system of separate exchange rates for capital and current transactions, as long practised in Belgium and now introduced in France, represents a metamorphosis of the capital controls technique in the direction of flexible exchange rates since the capital rate is allowed to vary. As compared with quantitative controls over capital, it represents a tremendous advance. Since the capital rate affects capital flows of almost all kinds—except for those closely associated with current transactions—and since it exercises a uniform degree of pressure on inflows and outflows, encouraging the one and discouraging the other, it attains a given effect on the balance of payments with less violent interference with particular types of flow. Partly for this reason, and partly because dividing transactions into two categories is a less exacting task than quantitative regulation of each type of transaction, it calls for a less elaborate administrative machinery than the usual type of comprehensive capital control. Like the latter, however, though to a lesser extent, the dual-rate system is subject to gaps and to evasion, and when dealing with strong disruptive flows may have to be supplemented by banking regulations relating to convertible balances and by regulation of trade credit. It affects capital flows in two ways—in the long run by creating a discrepancy between the exchange rate at which capital itself is transferred in one direction and the exchange rate at which the income from that capital will be transferred in the other direction, and in the short run by generating expectations or uncertainties regarding the future movements of the capital rate itself. Since the net capital flow passing through the capital-exchange market will depend on the amount of intervention carried out by the authorities, it provides an instrument for regulating that flow that is both flexible and precise. Like other systems resting on a foundation of exchange controls, it is most effective when dealing with genuinely temporary capital flows, particularly those of a speculative character. And like all such systems, it carries certain dangers of interfering with current transactions, particularly those relating to tourism.

EXCHANGE-RATE FLEXIBILITY

Most radical of all the remedies for disruptive capital flows is flexibility in the spot exchange rate. More than any type of capital control, rate, or fiscal incentive, it affects all types of capital movements. It reverses the course of disequilibrating and encourages equilibrating speculation. However, its effectiveness in dealing with disruptive flows may be bought at a high price in terms of instability of demand for foreign trade goods, or even in demand conditions generally, though the independence of monetary policy which it confers should facilitate stabilizing counter-measures. Partly for these reasons, countries are in practice loath to allow their exchange rates to float freely and, as we have recently had occasion to confirm, seek to control them by exchange-market intervention in the national interest. But complete national autonomy in the control of exchange rates is open to abuse from an international standpoint. Therefore, the tendency of official opinion at the present time is to favor exchange flexibility only within limits, specifically through wider margins of variation round a par value which can itself be changed. This technique, it is believed, will not only serve to buffer disequilibrating capital flows but will facilitate par value changes in the case of more enduring payments disequilibria. Since in fact many, if not most, disruptive capital flows are associated with the presence of fundamental disequilibrium, it is a particularly valuable feature of this technique for dealing with disruptive flows that it facilitates par value changes.

CONCLUDING REMARKS

From the catalogue of measures that I have somewhat pedantically ploughed through it will be clear that there is no lack of instruments —that there is, indeed, a somewhat embarrassing multiplicity of them— for dealing with disruptive capital flows.

Everyone will have his favorite approaches. My own preference is for those that operate through market mechanisms. The techniques that seem to me particularly worthy of further development are : first, the use of more flexible fiscal arrangements for the conduct of domestic cyclical policy allowing greater weight to be given to international considerations in determining interest-rate policy ; second, the use of measures of official financing that do not involve substantial variations in world reserves, such as borrowing by deficit countries from official or private lenders in surplus countries and official forward-market intervention ; third, where resort is had to exchange control, its application in the form of dual exchange rates, supplemented when necessary by controls over banking positions ; and last, but not least, the use of wider exchange-rate margins, or even, where there is serious uncertainty about the underlying balance-of-payments position, transitional floating rates.

In view of the multiplicity of policy instruments that is available for meeting this problem of volatile capital, and given the extent to which the appropriate use of these instruments is affected not only by the precise circumstances of the situation but also by ideological attitudes towards their use both of which vary from country to country and from time to time, the best practical rule could be for each country to have the responsibility to protect itself or not to protect itself against disequilibrating flows by methods of its own choosing.

Many will feel a sense of dissatisfaction with the proposition that it is up to each country to decide for itself what it will do about disruptive capital flows and will cast about for possible specific forms of intergovernmental cooperation in dealing with such flows. I must confess to being quite skeptical on this matter. The achievement of international cooperation and mutual adjustment is beset by many difficulties arising out of divergencies in economic interest, ideological preferences and political inhibitions, and is therefore a very time-consuming task. If it is as difficult to organize joint action to deal with basic trade and payments disequilibria that develop slowly over a period of years, as in recent years it has proved to be, it is hard to believe that cooperative action can be improvised with sufficient promptness to deal with such sudden and transitory phenomena as disruptive capital flows. Countries that prefer not to use exchange-control techniques to protect their own payments equilibrium, are unlikely to do so, as is sometimes suggested, to backstop the exchange controls of other countries. The exercise of joint international controls over Euro-currency transactions, which is another favorite candidate as a field for cooperative endeavor, also appears to be beset with very great difficulties—but these can be discussed in connection with Mr. Swoboda's paper. International coordination of interest policies at first appears a more promising field for international cooperation if only because short-term interest rates are predominantly under the control of central banks which have a habit of consulting together at fairly frequent intervals. But not only is it technically hard to determine what relative structure of international interest rates would be conducive to short-term payments equilibrium at any given time, it would also be politically very difficult, in view of differences in the cyclical situation in different countries, to obtain agreement regarding the absolute level of such rates. Moreover, many countries would be reluctant, for good reason, to divert monetary policy entirely from the pursuit of internal stabilization to that of external balance, and would prefer to preserve the independence of their monetary policies while adopting some of the other methods for keeping external payments in short-term equilibrium that have been discussed in this paper.

There is, however, a policy for dealing with capital flows which is international in its essence and offers an appropriate field for international cooperation, namely the provision of intergovernmental financing, especially of the sort that gives rise as a by-product to variations in international reserves. In so far as such financing is provided by the Fund or by the BIS, the provision of financing facilities is, from the start, under international control. This is less true of such assistance as is provided bilaterally through swaps and other credit arrangements and there is scope for an improvement in international organization in this field of a kind that would take due account of repercussions in the supply of international reserves.

In addition there is scope for cooperative action in arriving at criteria to which national policies regarding international capital flows should conform in the general interest.

First, as an example of such action it is suggested that any measures adopted with respect to capital flows should be equilibrating, or at least neutral, from a payments standpoint, certainly not disequilibrating.[1] Second, in the special case of the United States, so long as the dollar remains the principal reserve and intervention currency, and is incon-

[1] A difficult problem arises in this connection with respect to the European Economic Community. It is difficult to combine arrangements to control capital flows between each member country and the outside world in the interest of payments equilibrium of that member with freedom of capital flows among the members of the Community. On the one hand, it follows from the economic theory of the second best that it would be uneconomic to permit freedom of capital movement within the Community if capital flows between the outer world and different parts of the Community were subject to differential incentives. On the other hand, to subject such flows to a uniform degree of encouragement or discouragement could involve making them equilibrating in some member countries, disequilibrating in others. The ideal solution doubtless would be for exchange rates within the Community to be sufficiently flexible to preserve a uniform degree of hardness or softness in the currencies of all member countries. But the received doctrine of narrow margins and relative exchange-rate rigidity within the Community could make this very difficult to achieve. This difficulty cannot be removed by greater exchange-rate flexibility of the Community as a whole vis-à-vis the outer world. Nor can it be removed, though it can be disguised, by the provision of balance-of-payments financing from surplus to deficit members of the Community.

vertible, an attitude of "laissez passer" so far as capital is concerned, though very natural, is scarcely fair to the rest of the world which has to finance or check the resulting flows ; in this case active measures of an equilibrating kind would seem to be required. Third, and most important, capital control, to the extent that it is undertaken for balance-of-payments reasons, should not be allowed to prevent basic economic adjustment indefinitely. Any long-continued resort to reserve movements or the issuance of reserve liabilities, or to other forms of special financing, or to fiscal/monetary policy mixes that distort investment or savings incentives, or to the active use of capital restrictions, or any long-continuance of discounts or premia in capital exchange rates constitute *prima facie* evidence of fundamental disequilibrium and should be taken into account by international authorities concerned with the assessment of appropriate exchange rates.

Eurodollars and the World Money Supply: Implications and Control

10

Alexander K. SWOBODA *
Graduate Institute of International Studies

I. INTRODUCTION

Over the past five years, most industrialized countries have experienced a substantial rise in the rate of inflation, a large increase in money supply, and a rapid accumulation of dollar reserves (except for the United States, of course). At the same time, the Eurodollar market has grown at an unabated pace while the magnitude and variance of short-term capital flows has increased.

A few figures may help put these developments in perspective. The average annual percentage rise in the consumer price index for the OECD countries increased rapidly after 1966 : whereas the average annual rate of increase for the 1959-1969 period was only 2.9 per cent, it rose to 4 per cent in 1968, to 5 per cent in 1969, and to 5.7 per cent in 1970 (first quarter 1969 to first quarter 1970).[1] Moreover, the United States wholesale price index rose by only roughly 1 per cent per annum from 1953 to 1967 while from 1965 to the first quarter of 1970 it rose by some 14 per cent—and other industrialized countries' wholesale indices (indicators of traded goods prices) moved in sympathetic fashion.[2] Using

---

* I am indebted to Helmut W. Mayer who pointed out, in correspondence, a serious mistake in my original argument and whose comments have helped clarify the exposition. I hasten to add that he would probably disagree with several of my interpretations and that these, as well as any remaining errors of logic, are my own. The algebra on which later parts of the present paper is based is developed explicitly in part of a separate paper tentatively entitled "Gold, Dollars, Eurodollars and the World Stock of Bank Liabilities".

[1] Source : OECD, *Inflation : The Present Problem,* report by the Secretary General, Paris, December 1970, Table I, p. 59.

[2] Figures given in Ronald I. McKinnon, *Monetary Theory and Controlled Flexibility in the Foreign Exchanges,* Princeton, Essays in International Finance, No. 84, April 1971, especially pp. 21-27.

IMF definitions, Elaine Goldstein has constructed a money supply (M_1) series that aggregates together the money supplies of the 14 industrial countries. She finds that, for the period 1964-I to 1970-IV, the annual rate of growth in the 14-country aggregate was 8.1 per cent, a weighted average of the U.S. (5.8 per cent) and other 13 countries (10.3 per cent) rates. For the same period, she finds that the annual rate of growth of reserves of the 13 countries amounted to 6 per cent and that of the United States to -2.5 per cent. [3]

Turning to the Eurodollar market, the 1971 Annual Report of the BIS estimates that dollar assets and liabilities of reporting European banks stood at 60,370 million and 58,700 million, respectively, at the end of December 1970. This represents a 572 per cent increase in assets and a 508 per cent increase in liabilities over their values in December 1964. More significant from our point of view is the increase in dollar assets and liabilities to non-banks. Over the period December 1966 to December 1970, dollar liabilities to non-banks increased from 4,130 to 11,240 million (or by 172 per cent) and dollar assets vis-à-vis non-banks increased from 2,100 to 11,850 million (or by 464 per cent). [4] Moreover, the BIS data indicates that changes in the net foreign currency position vis-à-vis non-residents of the commercial banks of various countries can be quite pronounced leading to large changes in the monetary base. This variability reflects, of course, the volatility of short-term capital flows, one main channel of which is the Euro-currency market. [5]

These stylized facts of recent international economic relations suggest that inflation tends to become generalized in an integrated world economy and that its rate will be partly determined by the rate of growth of money supplies in the world. In addition, it would appear that capital flows, especially of the Eurodollar variety, can contribute substantially to the spread of inflation from country to country. Finally, one may well ask whether the growth of the Eurodollar market does not reflect that market's deposit-creation potential and thus contributes to an actually or potentially "uncontrollable" increase in the world's money supply. Indeed,

---

[3] These figures are taken from an unpublished paper by Elaine Goldstein, "Growth of an Aggregate Money Supply : 1964-1970".

[4] For the Eurodollar figures, see Bank for International Settlements, *Forty-First Annual Report,* Basle, June 1971, especially p. 161. See also, the *Fortieth Annual Report,* Basle, June 1970, p. 151.

[5] For documentation of the increasing magnitude and volatility of short-term capital flows see the paper of J. Marcus Fleming, "The Problem of Disruptive Capital Flows", prepared for this conference.

these are precisely the questions raised by Governor Carli in a recent article on the Eurodollar market: [6]

> "... there is no system of restraints set up by monetary authorities on the operation of this market, which is thus theoretically capable of expanding itself without any limits except discretionary fractional reserves ... it is a mechanism which transmits and amplifies inflationary pressures operating inside the U.S. It has also been argued that, by facilitating the transfer of funds from one market to another, the Eurodollar can hinder domestic monetary policies outside the U.S. ... It appears clear then that in the future an effective control over the process of money creation must be extended to cover funds created by the Eurodollar, and to be more general, the Eurocurrency market."

This paper seeks to provide some tentative answers to these questions at an analytical level. In the first part, I examine briefly the contribution of capital flows to the spread of inflation and the control of the money supply from the point of view of an individual relatively "small" country. The argument of this first part will be presented quite succinctly since it has been developed in more detail elsewhere [7] and since controllability of an individual country's money stock is discussed mainly as background for the investigation of controllability of the world money stock in the second part of the paper. That second part defines the world money supply as the sum of the money supplies in the hands of the residents of various countries and makes use of (overly) simplified two-country models of the international financial system to discuss the implications of the Eurodollar market for the growth and control of the world's money stock.

II. EURODOLLARS AND NATIONAL MONEY STOCK

Inflation, in a world where capital does *not* move across boundaries, will nevertheless spread from country to country. For simplicity, consider the case of a small country under fixed exchange rates. Suppose that an initial equilibrium in all markets is disturbed by inflation abroad. Prices of tradable goods will start rising (because of arbitrage in goods at the fixed exchange rate). This increase in prices tends to create an excess demand for non-traded goods and for money. In the absence of policy

---

[6] Guido Carli, "Eurodollars: A Paper Pyramid", *Banca Nazionale del Lavoro Quarterly Review,* No. 97, June 1971, pp. 95-109. The quotations are from p. 98, p. 99, and p. 107.

[7] See, for instance, Alexander K. Swoboda, "Monetary Policy under Fixed Exchange Rates: Effectiveness, the Speed of Adjustment and Proper Use", *Economica,* Vol. XL, No. 158, May 1973, pp. 136-154.

intervention, prices of domestic goods start to increase as does the money stock in the hands of the public under the monetary influence of an emerging trade surplus. In the end, the price of domestic goods should, other things equal, tend to increase by the same percentage as that of traded goods, re-establishing equilibrium relative prices. Monetary policy, however, can moderate, at least for a time, the rise in the price of domestic goods by preventing the money supply in the hands of the public from expanding in step with the payments surplus. That is, the central bank can sterilize the monetary impact of the payments surplus, for instance through open-market sales of bonds, thus maintaining the excess demand for money and reducing that for domestic goods. The required rate of the sterilization operations is equal to the trade surplus. The latter will disappear only when domestic goods prices and the money supply have been allowed to rise.

The high interest sensitivity of capital flows through the Eurodollar market makes this sterilization policy much more difficult. For as the central bank tries to prevent the rise in the domestic money supply the resulting excess demand for money puts upward pressure on domestic rates of interest, thus attracting capital from abroad. The payments surplus is larger than when capital is immobile since a capital inflow must now be added to the trade surplus. Sterilization of the monetary impact of the payments surplus requires a much higher rate of open-market sales of bonds. As a matter of fact, the authorities may simply run out of bonds to sell, and would then either have to abandon sterilization or find substitutes for open-market operations.[8]

Note also that capital mobility will serve to re-establish more rapidly the equilibrium distribution of reserves in the world economy after a disturbance and in the absence of policy intervention. To take our previous example again, suppose a once-and-for-all rise in all foreign prices. In the absence of official intervention, this disturbance should lead to a re-distribution of reserves towards our small country and a consequent rise in its money supply (and domestic goods prices). The rate at which this re-distribution occurs is equal to the payments surplus of the small country ; with capital mobility this rate is much larger than when no capital movements take place.

In the preceding analysis, capital movements were seen as an instrument through which inflationary impulses originating in the goods and services market abroad get transmitted more speedily to individual (small) countries. Some analysts have diagnosed instability in the capital account

[8] A substitute to open-market operations is to induce commercial banks to absorb in their portfolios the foreign-exchange assets that would otherwise flow to the central bank. This is one of the goals of the German Bundesbank's policy of offering commercial banks special swap rates.

itself as the main potential or actual source of inflation for a small country. Suppose, for instance, that a sudden autonomous net inflow of Eurodollars into some "small" country occurs. This leads to a surplus, an increase in high-powered money, and a multiple expansion of the money supply and inflation—or so it is argued. Whereas such spurts of inflation may occur in the short run, rising prices in the small country should rapidly lead to a *trade* deficit, especially when the ratio of traded to non-traded goods is high, and falling interest rates should moderate the increase in capital inflow. Once payments equilibrium is re-established, the price level may be higher than before but will no longer tend to rise.

In the above example, a "disruptive" capital movement leads to opposite movements in trade and capital accounts, contrary to the usual criterion used to judge the disruptiveness of capital movements. Moreover, in the example of inflation originating in the trade account, the capital movement that re-establishes the equilibrium distribution of reserves—and in that sense is equilibrating—reinforces the trade surplus. On the basis of these observations, one is tempted to argue that disruptive capital movements are disruptive mainly to offsetting operations of central banks that attempt to maintain a stock of money that is incompatible with payments equilibrium.[9] In other words, capital flows are disruptive to the attempt to use monetary policy for internal balance under fixed exchange rates. One exception to this argument must be stated : when speculation as to a parity change sets in, the leads and lags mechanism will tend to make capital and trade accounts move in the same direction (even though exchange-rate and income effects would still tend to make the two accounts move in opposite directions).

The main implications of this section, then, are the importance of control of the money stock in the hands of the public for counter-cyclical and payments policy purposes on one hand, and the tendency of the equilibrium distribution of reserves to be established rapidly in a world of high capital mobility—as embodied in interest-sensitive Eurodollar flows—on the other hand.

III. EURODOLLARS AND THE WORLD MONEY SUPPLY

When capital mobility is high and exchange rates are fixed, inflation spreads rapidly and money is redistributed fairly quickly from one country to another through payments imbalances. An important determinant of

[9] That is, attempting to keep the money stock above the level compatible with payments equilibrium results in both a trade and capital account deficit, and vice-versa for neutralization policy.

tend to create a deficit in the United States. As reserves flow from the United States to Europe, the money supply of the first country decreases, that of the second country increases. If $m_1 = m_2$, the rate of decrease is equal to the rate of increase, and the redistribution of gold does not modify the initial increase in M_w, namely, m_1A_1. Algebraically, the loss of reserves of the United States means that α G decreases which implies that the redistribution of gold reinforces the impact effect if $m_2 > m_1$, and vice-versa if $m_1 > m_2$.

Our analysis so far has enabled us to determine the impact effect of changes in A_1 and A_2 on the world money supply and the final effect when $m_1 = m_2$. However, we are unable to specify the effect on each country's money supply unless we can specify the effect of changes in A_1 and A_2 on the distribution of gold reserves more exactly. This can be done by postulating an equilibrium distribution of the world money supply. Suppose, for instance, that payments equilibrium requires that the proportion of country l's money supply in the world money supply be β, that is, that we have $M_1 = \beta M_w$. Under a wide variety of standard assumptions as to the nature of the demand for money and of the international adjustment process, β can be shown to be related to the proportion of country l's money income in world money income, both being expressed in the same currency.[11] Then, one can show that an increase in a central bank's domestic assets leads to a loss of reserves that is inversely proportional to the country's equilibrium share in the world money supply. The reason for this is simply that the reserve flows work to re-establish the initial distribution of the world's money stock.

Two features of this gold-standard model are worth noting. First, given the world gold stock and the domestic assets of one of the two countries, the total world money supply cannot be increased indefinitely by expansion of the other country's domestic assets. For the latter country would eventually run out of reserves if it pursued a systematically expansionary monetary policy. Second, the gold-standard system is a basically symmetric system. For an increase in A_1 has exactly the same effect as an increase in A_2 on M_1, on M_2, and on M_w, independently of whether

[11] Postulating an equilibrium distribution of the world money supply is far from arbitrary. Such an equilibrium distribution, β, can be derived from both classical and Keynesian short-run models and it can be shown to be invariant to money supply changes though not to fiscal policy. On this, see the paper by this author quoted in footnote 7 and Alexander K. Swoboda and Rudiger Dornbush, "International Adjustment, Policy, and Monetary Equilibrium in a Two-Country Model", to appear in M. B. Connolly and A. K. Swoboda, Editors, *International Trade and Money* (London, George Allen & Unwin, 1973).

$m_1 = m_2$ or not.[12] That is, redistribution of gold through the monetary mechanism of payments adjustment insures that monetary policy (here open-market operations) has the same effect on each money supply, whichever country it originates in. Changes in money stocks of individual countries become internationalized in a symmetric fashion. Both the limit on the expansion of the world money stock and this symmetry are lost when one moves to a dollar standard or introduces the Eurodollar market.

2. *A Dollar Standard*

Consider now the case where Europe's Central Bank holds dollars and not gold as reserves. Suppose (somewhat unrealistically) that these dollar balances are held with the Federal Reserve System. Assume, also, that the system does *not* neutralize the effect of changes in these balances on reserves available to U.S. commercial banks. In terms of T-accounts we have the following system :

2. *Dollar Standard*

	FED		Commercial Banks	
United States	*Assets*	*Liabilities*	*Assets*	*Liabilities*
	A_1	R_1	R_1	M_1
		D_2	L_1	
	Central Bank		Commercial Banks	
Europe	*Assets*	*Liabilities*	*Assets*	*Liabilities*
	A_2	R_2	R_2	M_2
	D_2		L_2	

where : D_2 = dollar reserves of the European Central Bank held at the FED.

The expression for the world money supply—which is easily derived from the balance sheets above—now becomes :

$$(3) \quad M_w = m_1A_1 + m_2A_2 + D_2(m_2 - m_1).$$

[12] This and other statements in the text can be proved by using balance-sheet identities to derive reduced-form expressions for the world money supply and differentiating those with respect to A_1 or A_2. These formal proofs are given in the separate paper mentioned in the introductory note.

As before, the size of the world money supply depends on the domestic assets held by the two central banks, the deposit multipliers, and the distribution of world reserves—in this case simply the dollar assets held by the European Central Bank. It can be shown that the conclusions to be drawn in this case are, with one exception, exactly the same as those reached in the gold standard case. Again, the same increase in the world and individual country money stocks results from an increase in either A_1 or A_2 and an increase in one central bank's domestic assets leads to a loss of reserves inversely proportional to the country's equilibrium share in the world money supply. The one difference with the gold standard case is that no upper limit is set on the world money supply by the constancy of A_2. The Federal Reserve can increase its holdings of domestic assets, and hence the world money supply, without running into a foreign-exchange constraint, whereas Europe's Central Bank cannot.

Further asymmetries would be introduced in the system were Europe's Central Bank to hold all or part of its reserves with U.S. commercial banks. This second version of the dollar standard, where dollar reserves are kept with U.S. commercial banks, corresponds fairly closely to current practice : foreign official dollar balances at the FED are relatively small and fairly constant ; moreover, foreign official holdings of U.S. treasury bills can be assimilated analytically to holdings of dollar deposits at U.S. commercial banks.

In terms of T-accounts, and supposing that Europe's Central Bank holds all its international reserves with U.S. commercial banks, simply relabel D_2, D_2^* and switch it from the liabilities of the FED to those of U.S. commercial banks. The expression for the world money supply becomes :

$$(4) \quad M_w = m_1A_1 + m_2A_2 + (m_2 - 1)\, D_2^*.$$

Given the distribution of reserves, the *impact* effect of an increase in A_1 or A_2 is the same as before. This has led some analysts to argue on the basis of T-accounts that it makes no essential difference whether European dollar reserves are held at the FED or with, say, Chase Manhattan. This is incorrect for it neglects the impact of changes in A_1 or A_2 on reserves D_2^*. An increase in A_1 creates a United States deficit and hence increases D_2^*, whereas an increase in A_2 creates a European deficit and hence decreases D_2^*. Therefore, an increase in the domestic assets of the United States increases the world money supply by more than under the gold standard or the first version of the dollar standard, and an increase in European domestic assets increases the world money supply by less than previously. Finally, if Europe's Central Bank holds its reserves partly at the FED and partly with U.S. commercial banks, a switch of its deposits from the former to the latter will increase the world money supply.

These asymmetries stem from the fact that high-powered money in one country (European reserves in U.S. commercial banks) competes with low-powered money in another (U.S. commercial bank liabilities). A 100 dollar increase in the European Central Bank's deposits with U.S. commercial banks decreases the money supply in the hands of the U.S. public by only $100, given A_1, while it leads to an increase in Europe's money supply that is a multiple of $100.

The multiple expansion of the world stock of bank liabilities to the public due to Eurodollar growth is based on similar considerations. For, in the Eurodollar market, the dollar reserves of Eurobanks are high-powered money to the latter but compete with low-powered money in the United States. We are ready, then, to incorporate the Eurodollar market into our analysis.

3. *A Eurodollar System*

A simple way of incorporating the Eurodollar market in our schematic two-country models is to add Eurodollar deposits to the liabilities of European commercial banks. For simplicity, these deposits are counted as part of the "money" held by European residents.[13] The dollar reserves held against these deposits by Eurobanks are then added to the reserve assets of Eurobanks and to the deposit liabilities of U.S. commercial banks. This simple Eurodollar subsystem can be grafted on either the gold-standard model or onto one or the other version of the dollar standard. The resulting systems of T-accounts are as follows :

3. *Gold Standard with Eurodollars*

	FED		Commercial Banks	
United States	*Assets*	*Liabilities*	*Assets*	*Liabilities*
	G_1	R_1	R_1	M_1
	A_1		L_1	DEB
	Central Bank		Commercial Banks	
Europe	*Assets*	*Liabilities*	*Assets*	*Liabilities*
	G_2	R_2	R_2	M_2^1
	A_2		DEB	ED
			L_2	

[13] As mentioned in the list of simplifying assumptions stated at the beginning of Section III, this by-passes the question of what proportion of Eurodollar deposits should be counted as money (versus quasi-money).

4. *Dollar Standard with Eurodollars*

	FED		Commercial Banks	
United States	*Assets*	*Liabilities*	*Assets*	*Liabilities*
	A_1	R_1	R_1	M_1
		D_2		DEB
				D_2^*

	Central Bank		Commercial Banks	
Europe	*Assets*	*Liabilities*	*Assets*	*Liabilities*
	A_2	R_2	R_2	M_2^1
	D_2		DEB	ED
	D_2^*		L_2	

where : ED = dollar deposits of the non-bank public with European commercial banks, DEB = dollar reserves of European commercial banks held with U.S. commercial banks, and M_2^1 = European currency deposits of the non-bank public at European commercial banks.

Denoting the reserve ratio kept by European commercial banks against their dollar liabilities by r_d and the inverse of this ratio by m_d, it is an easy matter to modify the world money supply formulae given above to take the Eurodollar subsystem into account. All that needs to be done is to add the term $(m_d - 1)$ DEB to each expression. That is, a $100 increase in the dollar assets held by Eurobanks with U.S. commercial banks adds, *other things equal,* $(m_d - 1)$ 100 dollars to the world money supply. The basis of this additional term is easy to understand. Other things equal, an increase of $100 in Eurobank dollar assets leads to a $m_d \cdot \$100$ increase in Eurodollar deposits of the non-bank public but reduces the dollar deposits at U.S. commercial banks available to the non-bank public by $100, thus expanding the money supply in the hands of the non-bank public by $(m_d - 1)$ $100, a multiple of the initial $100 increase in dollar assets of Eurobanks.

This analysis, however, is deficient in at least two respects. It does not specify the factors that determine the magnitude of DEB and assumes other things, in particular the distribution of foreign-exchange reserves, equal when in fact they are not.

An examination of the T-accounts above helps to distinguish several sources of an increase in DEB. On one hand, an increase in the demand for Eurodollar deposits (ED) by the public will increase Eurobanks' demand for dollar reserves (DEB). For a given initial world money supply, such an increase may originate in a switch to Eurodollar deposits

(ED) either from dollars held with U.S. commercial banks (M_1) or from European currency deposits (M_2^1). On the other hand, an increase in DEB may originate in any change that increases the supply of total reserves (DEB + R_2) to European commercial banks. The source of this increase in total reserves may be either an increase in domestic credit creation by Europe's Central Bank (an increase in A_2) or an increase in its foreign-exchange reserves (G_2, D_2, or D_2^*), the latter possibly due to an increase in A_1. The way in which the increase in total reserves of European commercial banks is distributed between holdings of dollars (DEB) and holdings of reserves at the European Central Bank (R_2) depends on the public's preferences on how an increase in its total deposits at European commercial banks should be divided between its components ED and M_2^1.

As such switches and changes occur, however, other things will not stay equal. The expansion and contraction of individual money supplies will tend to create payments imbalances which in turn further modify the impact effects of disturbances. These complications do not mean, however, that nothing precise can be said about the effects of deposit-switches or of changes in domestic credit creation on the stock of money of the world and of individual countries. For the concept of an equilibrium distribution of the world money supply and the specification of the public's preferences as between different types of deposits enables us to reach conclusions that are quite precise.

As before, payments equilibrium requires that the money supply in the hands of United States non-bank residents stand in a proportion β to that in the hands of European residents. A general way of specifying the deposit preferences of the public is to assume that U.S. residents wish to hold a given proportion of their total deposits in the Eurodollar market and that European residents hold a given fraction of their total deposits in that same market. For simplicity, I shall assume in what follows that only European non-bank residents hold Eurodollar deposits in a given proportion (say, Ω) of their total deposits ($M_2 = M_2^1 + ED$). A precise algebraic formulation based on these assumptions is possible but will not be presented here. The essence of the results that can be derived from such a formulation, however, can be stated verbally and explained intuitively.

Consider, first, the effect of an increase in the domestic assets of the Federal Reserve System (A_1), brought about, for instance, by open-market purchases of bonds. The impact effect, before reserves are redistributed, is simply to raise the U.S. money supply by a multiple (m_1) of the increase in A_1. This, however, disturbs the equilibrium distribution of the world money supply and leads to an outflow of foreign-exchange reserves towards Europe. On the one hand, this outflow moderates the initial expansion of the American money supply (by a larger amount under a gold standard than under a dollar standard in which all or part of European foreign-exchange reserves are held with U.S. commercial banks). On the other hand, it increases the monetary base of the European Central Bank (A_1 + foreign-exchange reserves). This puts reserves at the disposal of commercial banks and the European-currency component of Europe's money stock (M_1^1) expands. At it does, however, the public also attempts to build up its Eurodollar deposits against which European commercial banks will want to hold dollar reserves in New York. Though the growth of Eurodollar deposits does not absorb any of the increase in the domestic-currency reserves (R_2) of European commercial banks, its impact on DEB moderates slightly the expansion in the money supply in the hands of U.S. residents (M_1) and, hence, the foreign-exchange gain of Europe's Central Bank. The end result depends on which system the Eurodollar market has been grafted on.

Essentially, Eurodollar deposits play a role similar to that of dollar deposits of the European Central Bank with U.S. commercial banks. The dollar deposits of European *commercial* banks (DEB) serve as a base for the Eurodollar deposits of the non-bank public just as the dollar balances of the European Central Bank (D_2^*) serve as a base for European-currency deposits of the public in the absence of the Eurodollar market. The potential for multiple expansion in both cases stems from the fact that D_2^* or DEB are subtractions from low-powered money in Europe. Assuming all reserve ratios to be the same to abstract from asymmetries arising from differences in individual deposit multipliers, we can conclude that the Eurodollar market tends to amplify monetary disturbances if grafted on to the gold standard or onto a dollar standard where Europe's Central Bank holds its international reserves at the Federal Reserve. However, the monetary expansion generated (though not the change in official reserves) by an increase in A_1 or A_2 will be the same under a dollar standard where Europe's Central Bank holds all its reserves with U.S. commercial banks, whether the Eurodollar market exists or not.[14] For, an increase in, say, A_1, creates a disequilibrium that is eliminated by an increase in D_2^* and in DEB, the two increases acting in identical fashion on the world money supply.

To summarize, monetary expansion in the United States leads to a larger expansion in the world money supply than it otherwise would if either the European Central Bank holds its reserves with U.S. commer-

[14] I had originally claimed that existence of the Eurodollar market increases the world money supply multiplier even in this case. This is the mistake that Helmut Mayer pointed out in correspondence.

cial banks or when the Eurodollar market exists. If only European residents hold Eurodollar deposits the expansion will be the same whether the Eurodollar market exists or not if all European international reserves are held with commercial banks. With this exception (which is quite relevant in practice), the extent of the additional monetary expansion due to the existence of the Eurodollar system depends positively on the ratio of Eurodollars relative to other deposits kept by the public, and inversely on the size of the United States relative to Europe (as reflected in β) and on the reserve ratio kept by Eurobanks against their dollar liabilities. Finally, note that if U.S. residents also hold a proportion of their total deposits in the Eurodollar market, its expansive powers are increased even if all European official reserves are kept with U.S. commercial banks. For, such holdings are similar in their effect to a decrease in β, the share of U.S. money in world money.

Even when the Eurodollar system is taken into account, the final effect of an increase in A_2 on M_w, M_1, M_2^1, and ED is the same as that of an increase in A_1 unless Europe's Central Bank holds part or all of its reserves at U.S. commercial banks, thus introducing asymmetries in the system. This may seem surprising at first but is readily explained by the response of foreign-exchange reserves to changes in A_1 and A_2, respectively. Consider the changes that occur in the sources of each country's monetary base (central bank assets). An increase in A_1 of $100 leads to an outflow of reserves of $(1 - \beta)$ $100 resulting in a *net* increase of β ($100) in the United States' monetary base and a net increase of $(1 - \beta)$ $100 in Europe's monetary base. On the other hand, an increase in A_2 of $100 leads to an outflow of reserves of β ($100) from Europe to the United States, leading to a *net* increase of $(1 - \beta)$ $100 in Europe's base and of β ($100) in the American base. The final net changes in monetary bases are the same in the two cases though the sequence of events will be quite different.

In addition to domestic monetary expansion, shifts in deposit preferences by the public can have a significant influence on the total world money stock and its distribution. Suppose, for instance, that European residents decide to hold a higher proportion of their monetary wealth in the Eurodollar market than before. This increase in the ratio Ω will lead to an increase in the world money supply even though the domestic assets of central banks remain the same unless the European Central Bank keeps all its reserves with U.S. commercial banks. The increase of dollar relative to European-currency deposits at European commercial banks liberates part of the European monetary base and this would tend to lead to an induced expansion of both Eurodollar and domestic currency deposits. In the United States, the money supply in the hands of United States' residents tends to decrease because of the induced increase in the New York dollar deposits of Eurobanks (DEB). However, the

Turning to shifts in deposits—changes (3) and (4) above,—an autonomous shift of deposits towards the Eurodollar market tends to increase the world money supply whatever its source, unless all European foreign-exchange reserves are kept with U.S. commercial banks. In that case, only a shift from New York deposits, but not from European-currency deposits, tends to increase the world money supply. In any event, when New York dollar balances are the source of the shift, European foreign-exchange reserves increase while, if the source is European-currency deposits, they decline.

Finally, in the cases where it occurs, the increase in the world money-supply multiplier attributable to the Eurodollar system depends on a number of readily identifiable factors. The increase will be the higher, the lower the reserves kept against Eurodollar deposits by Eurobanks, the lower the leakages from the Eurodollar system *(i.e.,* the higher the proportion of Eurodollar deposits to either European-currency deposits or U.S. dollar deposits), the "larger" Europe is relative to the United States, and the more European central banks keep foreign-exchange reserves in the Eurodollar market.

4. *Some Implications for Control*

The conclusions above have some obvious implications for the control of the long-run growth of the world money supply, on the one hand, and for that of short-run instability in monetary aggregates, on the other hand. The first of these concerns stems on one hand, from the possible multiplicative powers of the Eurodollar system and on the other hand, and more importantly, from the absence of limits imposed on dollar creation under a dollar standard ; the second from the combination of high multiplicative powers with instability of the deposit preferences of the public.

If deposit preferences are stable, the world money supply will still be a stable multiple (or function) of domestic credit expansion and of variations in outside international reserves of central banks, gold and SDRs. The problem is one of control of these magnitudes and not one of control of the Eurodollar market if stable growth of the world money supply is to be insured. If a secular and pathologic propensity towards over-expansion in domestic credit creation is diagnosed, one might well argue for a policy-engineered reduction of the multiplier applied to this expansion. Two obvious steps can be taken to effect such a reduction (or at least to prevent further increases). First, central banks should abstain from depositing their foreign-exchange reserves in the Eurodollar market. Second, they should keep their dollar reserves with the Federal Reserve System rather than with U.S. commercial banks, thereby also avoiding some undesirable asymmetries in the system.

A reduction in the world-money multiplier is also desirable on stability grounds when deposit preferences or national money multipliers are unstable. Some care must be taken in interpreting the word unstable. It is obvious that the multipliers specified in this paper will be functions of interest rates ; as long as they are stable functions of interest rates our conclusions will hold qualitatively. The multipliers that take interest-rate effects into account will simply be lower than those that neglect them. Instability, for our purposes, will be defined, instead, as autonomous variations in deposit preferences that do not reflect changes in interest rates induced by changes in the monetary base. The obvious example of instability in this sense is shifts in deposit preferences attendant to expectations of a currency crisis. A milder form of instability is due to seasonal strains arising, for instance, from year-end window-dressing operations. The problems that such instability pose are amplified by the existence of the Eurodollar system ; the result may well be sudden deflationary or inflationary tendencies spreading to the world economy as a whole instead of the milder realignments that would occur, for instance, in a more simple gold-standard world.

There is no easy solution to the problems posed by the volatility of deposit preferences. One obvious step, as mentioned above, is to moderate their repercussions by eliminating practices that tend to increase the Eurodollar multiplier. This step, however, is a matter of medium or long-run policy, not one of short-run policy. Co-ordinated intervention in the Eurodollar market at times of unusual strain—insofar as this strain reflects shifts in deposit preferences and not a liquidity squeeze due to price inflation in the world as a whole—constitutes another step in the right direction. This is exactly the policy that has been practiced, with a good deal of success, by a group of central banks in co-operation with the Bank for International Settlements. They intervene almost routinely at year-end, half-year and even quarterly, to deal with seasonal stringencies in the market—and less routinely during speculative crises—by channelling large amounts of funds to the Eurodollar market. In terms of our analysis, a decrease in Ω or a reflow of Eurodollar deposits to the U.S. commercial banking system is compensated by an increase in γ, the proportion of foreign-exchange reserves held in the Eurodollar market. Note that proper policy requires that this increase in γ be only temporary ; if permanent, it would serve to exacerbate the impact of further shifts in deposit preferences.

It is tempting to argue that the simplest way to deal with the instability problem is to control the Eurodollar market through exchange controls, quantitative credit ceilings, and so forth. The argument is incorrect. First, shifts in deposit preferences are symptoms of more serious illnesses of the system ; the proper policy is to deal with the sickness and not with the symptoms. Second, non-market controls might well aggravate the instability that they are supposed to eradicate. As ceilings on interest rates or on the foreign-exchange positions of banks, to take but two examples, are reached, sudden shifts in the location and currency denomination of deposits will tend to occur, aggravating rather than alleviating instability.[17]

To conclude, it should be pointed out that the impact of the Eurodollar market on the growth and stability of the world money stock has not reached huge proportions in practice—even though the problems it poses for individual countries are quite significant. From the vantage point of this paper, the relevant figure for Eurodollar deposits is the deposits in the hands of the non-bank public. These are much smaller than the total Eurodollar liabilities of Eurobanks, the total most often quoted. Second, the leakages from the Eurodollar system are quite large as indicated by low values of Ω, the ratio of Eurodollar assets of the public to their domestic-currency monetary assets. Nevertheless, the close interconnection between national monetary systems that is reflected in the Eurodollar market makes control of the world money supply a matter of international concern.

[17] For an obvious analogy, consider the effects of interest-rate ceilings imposed by regulation Q on both the United States money multiplier and on the Eurodollar market.

INDEX